Nelson's Guide to Florida Roses

Mark Nelson
of Nelsons' Florida Roses

with Hank Bruce

Waterview Press
Orlando

Waterview Press, Inc.
3208 East Colonial Drive
Orlando, Florida 32803

Copyright © 2003 by Mark Nelson and Hank Bruce. All rights reserved. No part of this book may be used or reproduced in any manner whatsoever without written permission of the publisher except in the case of brief quotations as part of articles and reviews. To reproduce excerpts or for other information, please contact the publisher.

June 2003
Manufactured in the United States of America
Distributed by Mickler's Books, Inc. • Oviedo, Florida 32765
www.micklers.com

Cover design by Jonathan Pennell
Photography by Tomi Jill Folk and Roger Kilgore

Library of Congress Cataloging-in-Publication Data will be furnished upon request

ISBN 1-883114-16-0

Dedication

This book is dedicated to my wife, Elizabeth Anne McKinnon Nelson and
To all of my roses: Sean, Anne, Clay, Elly and Kit; may you flourish.
You are my inspirations!

Acknowledgments

Growing roses in Florida for more than 25 years does not make me the expert. This book contains some of the experiences and wisdom from my father, B. P. Nelson and Uncle Earl Nelson. They planted in a twelve-year-old boy a lifelong passion for roses. As for growing roses the easy way, I guess I'm just a product of my generation, a Baby Boomer. My gratitude and thanks to Dad and Uncle Earl, and also to my grandparents Olin and Mable Nelson, brother Stephen, sister Kim and cousins Scott and Bryan Nelson. Our rose grower, Wilbert Chisholm, guided the twelve-year- old Mark through a lot of mistakes.

Many dealers provided insight into bringing quality roses to the public:

Phil Dubeau (Green Garden Nursery), Don & Nancy Mattson (Green Pak), Wayne Hibbs & Bucky Hibbs (Wayne Hibbs Farm & Garden), Don Jones (Jones Nursery), Phil Lukas (Lukas Nursery), Ric (Ric's Garden World), George & Terri Grimes (Grimes Produce), Richard Hardin (Hardin's Nursery), Fran Francisco (Blodgett Nursery, Bernie Peterson (Rockledge Gardens), Jim Scrivner (Scrivner's Nursery), Gene O'Conner (O'Conner's Flower Haven), Frank White (White's Nursery) and Linus Olson plus so many more.

Rosarians and experts in the field: Charles and Ada Alcott, Bruce Barney, Bob Bowden (Harry P. Leu Gardens), The Central Florida Rose Society, Jack Christmas, Jim and Dianne Giles, Ron and Shirley Kast, Randy Knight, Mrs. Nelsons' (Rose Garden dedicated in her name at Rollins College), Malcomb Manners, Tom McCubbin (Orange County Extension Service), Barbara Olbeck (author), Robert Vincent Simms (The Garden Rebel), Marty and Elaine Pawlikowski, Tom Wickman (Orange County Extension Service).

Some wonderful folks at Walt Disney World that we have had the pleasure of working with also deserve our thanks: Katie Moss Warner, Sam Lemheney, Ben Brogdon, Robin Esakof, Mark Maynes, Mark Krause, Laura Coar, Jessie Mack-Burns and Belinda Townsend.

Give Kids the World: They have used our roses to spread beauty and love for so many families. This is, after all, what roses are for. Special thanks to Henri Landwirth who has done so much.

Thanks also to my office staff: Louise, Dena, Paula, Christine and all of the employees at O. F. Nelson & Sons and Nelsons' Florida Roses.

Thanks also to Hank Bruce and Tomi Jill Folk for their help in putting this book together.

To all these people and to anyone I might have missed, my sincere and deepest gratitude.

Old Fashioned Rose
Rosa species

Contents

Introduction ix

Part 1: In the Rose Garden
Three Keys to the Rose Garden 1
How to Grow Roses in Florida 5
How to Kill a Rose 12
Using Roses in the Residential Landscape,
 Beyond the Rose Garden 14
Roses on Golf Courses and Commercial Landscaping ... 19

Part 2: The Nelsons' Roses Book of Lists
Carefree and Low Maintenance Roses for Your Consideration ... 23
Top Fragrant Roses for Florida 34
My Favorites by Color 35
Frequently Asked Questions 36
Roses, as American as Apple Pie, a quiz 42

Part 3: Beyond the Rose Garden
Using Roses as Cut Flowers 47
Roses Can Be Dried 49
Other Uses for Roses 50
Roses on the Dinner Table 52
Healing with Roses 60
Who Said That About Roses? a quiz 60

Part 4: Roses in Myth, Legend & History
Rose Myths and Legends 65
A Brief History of the King of Flowers 69
A Brief History of Roses in America 72
The Cherokee Rose 74
A Possible Dream, a Rose Supreme 76
Absolutely Useless Information, another quiz ... 78

Part 5: Defining the Rose
Dictionary of Rose Terms 81
Everything's Comin' Up Roses in the Music Industry ... 113

Introduction

Most folks who grow roses in Florida enjoy the color and fragrance and the almost mystic charm of these plants. They grow them with moderate effort and lots of success. That is, if they don't "fuss them to death." One gentleman complained to me that he just couldn't grow roses in Florida like he could in Michigan. He's right, because here we can enjoy the flowers twelve months a year, we don't have to use rose cones in the winter, prune them into oblivion or do battle with Japanese beetles. Yet the myth persists that roses are a difficult challenge here. They aren't labor intensive and demand far less attention than the family dog. Roses aren't expensive prima donnas that insist on the most expensive pampering a gardener can provide. A bed of blooming annuals, or the St. Augustine grass in your lawn, requires much more of your time and energy.

We're talking about roses for the fun of it

It's very true that life itself isn't problem free, and neither are roses. There are problems, but most of them can be avoided if you follow the suggestions in this book. Some growers, hobbyists and rose enthusiasts get so wrapped up in the *rules of rose cultivation* that they forget how to relax and enjoy their fascinating, intriguing and delightful roses.

The American gardener has been taught by the TV commercials, magazine ads and in-store displays to look for the problems, fear every bug, panic at the sight of a fallen leaf. Of course the solution is to rush out and buy an insecticide, herbicide or fungicide; engage in chemical warfare and not rest until the enemy is totally destroyed, along with every other living creature in the rose garden, back yard or lawn. No rose bush ever died from black spot, but millions have died from improperly used fertilizers, fungicides and pesticides. It's much easier to prevent problems than it is to solve them.

In the next few pages we will outline a program of rose care that gives you plenty of time to enjoy them. We will also make several suggestions about how roses can be used, experienced and shared. It's the versatility of the rose, its fascinating diversity and willingness of this dynamic plant to grow almost anywhere people do, that give it such a mystique.

The rose isn't just another pretty flower, it is the absolute symbol of beauty. The rose is a tradition with people that reaches back in time to the very beginnings of humanity. We may well have domesticated the rose before we domesticated the horse. The rose has such a deep traditional link with people all over the world that every continent, almost every nation in the northern hemisphere values and honors this dramatic plant.

They were grown by the Egyptians before the reign of Cleopatra. The Romans showered their heroes with rose petals.Wars were fought in the name of roses. They were the symbol of romance, the object of great expeditions, the basis for financial empires. Roses were valued by herbalists, clergy, kings and poets, not to mention FTD florists. Roses have appeared on postage stamps all over the world, been the subject of great art, expensive perfumes and even been declared the official national flower of the United States and many other nations. Today roses are grown everywhere but Antarctica.

We didn't include pages of color photos partly because of the cost of printing color. Most of the colorful picture books are printed in the Orient and we wanted to work with American publishers and printers. Also, there are lots of color catalogs, web pages and best of all, the living color of Nelsons' roses in the garden centers. We wanted to write a book devoted to having fun with roses as you grow them and live with them, not as a selection guide.

This little book is written in the hope that it can help to eliminate the fear of rose growing in Florida, open the door to the rose garden for you the reader, inspire you to explore and experiment in the garden and, above all, enjoy the company of roses. It is my hope that this will be the kind of book you pick up to read and enjoy, not just a place to turn when you have a problem.

We want you to grow roses for the fun of it. Thank you for including roses in your landscape and this book on your shelf.

Mark Nelson

*You can complain because roses have thorns,
or you can rejoice because thorns have roses.*

Ziggy

Part 1
In the Rose Garden

Three Keys to the Rose Garden

It matters not what goal you seek
Its secret here reposes:
You've got to dig from week to week
To get Results or Roses
                    Edgar Guest

Growing roses in Florida isn't an impossible dream. In fact, it's a gardening experience with opportunities unrivaled in many other parts of the country. In Florida we don't have to worry about protecting the plants from extreme cold, and we can enjoy our roses every day of the year. There are three simple keys that can unlock the door to successful rose growing for you.

The first key to successful roses in Florida is underground

Most people who have trouble growing roses "fuss them to death." First, we need to get over the idea that roses are a difficult challenge, an almost impossible task demanding an incredible amount of work. Rose growing here is a lot easier now than it was in the last century. The increase in your opportunity to have a successful rose garden today isn't the result of great advances in pesticides or the development of dynamic and rugged new varieties.

PART ONE

No, it's a matter of what's in the ground. The key is the rootstock. Most of the roses you find in garden centers or order from catalogs and web sites are grafted plants. The plant is a union of a scion and a stock. The stock is the root, and many varieties of rootstocks are used. They are selected for their ability to produce a vigorous plant in specific locations and under specific conditions. A rootstock can determine the size, number of blooms, hardiness and resistance to soilborne problems. In northern clay soils Rosa multiflora is the preferred choice. In the desert Southwest many growers use Dr. Huey, and this was popular in Florida for many years. Neither of these has proven to be the best choice for Florida, however.

The revolution in Florida rose growing began in 1848 in China. Robert Fortune discovered the Rosa fortuniana in Ningpo, China, and sent it to the Royal Horticultural Society in London. To confuse the subject, when this plant arrived in the United States early in the 20th century it was known as Double Cherokee. The American Rose Society states that Rosa fortuniana is believed to be a hybrid of the Cherokee rose (Rosa laevigata) and the Lady Banks rose (Rosa banksiae). Dr. Samuel McFadden at the University of Florida began working with this as a rootstock in the late 1950s and found that plants grafted onto Fortuniana produced at least twice the blooms of those grafted onto Dr. Huey. We began using Fortuniana about forty years ago; today we use it almost exclusively on all our varieties, even the old garden roses.

People frequently ask, "What's the big deal with Fortuniana rootstock? What makes it work so well in Florida?"
- It might be because it produces a fine, vigorous, deep root system ideal for our sandy soil.
- It might be because it is resistant to many kinds of nematodes. For the uninitiated, nematodes are sub-microscopic organisms that invade the roots, or other plant parts, and cause a general decline and eventual death of the plant.
- It might be because this rootstock is heat tolerant and thrives in the climate of even South Florida.
- It might be because it is drought tolerant and is able to support a rose bush that's expected to grow and bloom twelve months out of the year. Many roses and rootstocks require a period of dor-

mancy, Fortuniana doesn't.
- It might be because, in test after test, it out performs all other rootstocks used. For us, "The proof is in the pudding" and more than forty years of successful growing is all the proof we need.

It's unfortunate that many people purchase budget roses, plant them with great care, then watch them die. They decide that it's simply too difficult to grow roses in Florida and give up. This is unfortunate because for the most part this wasn't their failure; it was a matter of purchasing plants that were produced for other parts of the country. Many of the discount store roses and mail order roses are grown on rootstocks that are best for areas where there isn't a twelve-month growing season, sandy soil, nematodes, drought, extreme heat or some of the other elements that make Florida and the deep south a unique place to grow plants.

We, like the rose, bloom only when well grounded. —Anon

The second key to successful roses is to use varieties that are proven for our climate

Today we have literally thousands of varieties of roses. They range from the traditionals, to the hybrid teas, the floribundas, grandifloras, miniatures and shrub roses to varieties with clever marketing names. There are great native roses planted by nature on every continent in the northern hemisphere. There are roses designed by nature to grow in swamps, on mountain slopes, in dense forests and open prairies. There are manmade roses developed by hybridizers for color, fragrance, size of bloom and perceived marketability.

At Nelsons' Roses we have, in the past half century, grown more than 500 varieties, and trialed well over a thousand. Many were found unsuitable for our climate, even with the Fortuniana rootstock. As an example, many climbing roses don't bloom well in Florida, so we don't focus on them, but we do offer the best climbers for the Deep South. Many of the traditional roses that are popular in the British Isles or Europe are not able to enter a dormancy

PART ONE

period in Florida and fail to perform well. Some varieties are susceptible to the diseases and mildews that our high humidity encourages. Some of the old fashioned roses only bloom for a short period of time each year, and the average customer wants more from a rose garden.

Many discount store nurseries sell varieties that are beautiful and dynamic roses but which aren't the best choices for our climate. Mail-order catalogs and web site merchants also offer varieties of roses that might not perform well in your backyard.

Of course, we prefer that you plant Nelsons' roses, but to increase your chances for success, at least purchase plants that are Florida grown on Fortuniana rootstock. Beware of bargains; you usually get what you pay for. There is no need to purchase problems, regardless of the price.

> *Roses, oh they give us gifts a'plenty.*
> *Yesterday's faded bloom shines bright in every memory;*
> *while we inhale the beauty of today's flowers;*
> *and anxious await tomorrow's promise in buds not yet formed.*
>   Author unknown

The third key is the "fuss factor"

We started this chapter with the comment that many people fuss their roses to death. This is a fact. Because there has been so much information, misinformation, stupid information, advertising, and just plain lies written and spoken about roses, we are driven to the conclusion that there is better chance of winning the lottery than there is to get a rose bush to live long enough to produce a flower.

A lot of the "information" is really advertising. I saw a rose guide put out by a popular lawn and garden chemical company that had a spray schedule to keep your roses "safe and happy." This list of pesticides would have cost hundreds of dollars and required your engagement in chemical warfare almost daily. This guide wasn't written to produce "safe and happy" roses; it was written to sell their products. A professional grower who tried to follow such a schedule would go bankrupt. There is far more danger to you, your children, grandchildren and your roses in using too many insecticides, herbicides, fungicides, nematocides and fertilizers than there is in the appearance of an occasional bug, weed or spot on a leaf. The nematode threat was already almost eliminated as a problem by using the Fortuniana rootstock.

No rose bush ever died of Black Spot, but the overuse or improper use of fungicides has killed a multitude of roses. We kill with kindness when we overfeed, over spray and "fuss" too much. Relax and take the time to smell the roses rather than the Malathion.

> *It is only a tiny rosebud,*
> *a flower of God's design;*
> *But I cannot unfold the petals*
> *With these clumsy hands of mine.*
>
> — Anon

How To Grow Roses in Florida

You can find volumes, great and ponderous texts, that give detailed instructions on how to select, plant and care for roses. The process borders on cult-like ritual for many, with elements of masochism and self-imposed hard labor for others. Venturing into the rose garden of these mystical texts is akin to entering a fantasy land filled with evil monsters, beasts and demons, where your only defense is a series of incantations that sound like the names of pesticides. We find detailed instructions on how to select the site, prepare the bed, measure the soil nutrients and acidity. In processes reminiscent of medieval alchemy we are told how to prepare the proper soil mix for rose cultivation. Then there are the edicts on pruning; rules that must be followed to the letter. Failure to snip at the proper place and time would seem to mean certain death to your precious rose and a plague on your house as well.

Let's stop for a moment and take a reality check. Those grand pronouncements, those ritualized and detailed guides were probably not written for us Florida folks. They probably weren't written

PART ONE

for people who work for a living either. Let's get a couple of things straight right from the beginning.

> First, it's your back yard, your landscape, your rose garden. That means you are the boss. You can plant your roses any place you darn well please, any way you darn well please. Who am I to tell you what to do with your yard?
> Second, you bought this book because you thought you might be able to benefit from 40-plus years of commercial rose growing by the Nelson family. This book is a collection of suggestions that you might want to try, not rules that must be followed.

We are professional growers producing thousands of roses every year. We don't have time to fuss and pamper and coddle these plants. We work with some of the premier gardens in the state of Florida, Walt Disney World, Cypress Gardens, Harry P. Leu Gardens and others. One of the reasons we recommend roses for use on golf courses, commercial and business sites is because they don't demand nearly as much maintenance as annuals or turf grasses. I have been told that we don't know as much as a rose hobbyist because we only commercially grow roses in containers. From personal experience, I can tell you it is easier to grow roses in the ground than it is in pots in a nursery, especially in June, July and August.

Here is our list of simple suggestions

Before you purchase the plants, know where you are going to put them
- Roses do best in full sun, morning sun will guarantee that the leaves will dry early and there will be less danger of fungus problems. It is always easier to avoid a problem than it is to correct it. The basic rule for best growth is to provide a minimum of six hours of winter sun.
- The site should be well drained. Roses don't like wet feet. Having said that, with the Fortuniana rootstock there is far greater tolerance to temporary flooding.

- A site where there is good air circulation also helps to avoid fungus problems. A twelve-month growing season produces larger bushes. Spacing for most roses in Florida should be six feet apart rather than the four feet often recommended in the books.
- Plan for watering before planting. If you are going to use sprinklers, these liners should be in place before you begin to plant. Drip irrigation systems are far more efficient, easier to install and better for the roses.
- Visit a local botanic garden where there is an established rose display area and get to know the varieties in a mature planting, their growth habits, fragrance and ruggedness. If the plant is distressed in a professional setting, you may not want that variety in your back yard.
- Determine in your own mind the reason you are planting roses in this site. Is it for cut flowers, fragrance, erosion control, hedge, screen, curb appeal or personal pleasure? Make your selection accordingly.
- Give thought to the varieties, colors and types of roses you want to grow before you go to the garden center.

Purchasing the plants
- Because Nelson roses are always sold in our famous blue pot, we recommend that you look for that blue pot and the Nelson tag.
- Bargain plants offered as Saturday morning specials were usually produced for a different climate and stand little chance of thriving or surviving here.
- When you purchase a container grown rose that's in bloom you see exactly what you are getting. You know the leaf color, floral fragrance and color, and have an indication of growth habit.
- Stick to your guns and insist on the varieties on your list, especially if Nelsons' recommended it.

Rose hybridizers develop new roses, new colors and new names to sell every year. Our business is built on customer success; we're old fashioned that way. Unfortunately, many of these aren't suitable for our distinctive climate. We test hundreds of varieties, then grow and sell the best ones for Florida and Southern gardens.

PART ONE

Planting your chosen rose
- Dig a hole approximately 18" x 18"
- Gently remove the plant from the famous blue pot, being careful not to disturb the roots.
- Add to the hole at least one blue pot full of quality potting soil (not the 99 cent stuff), and mix with the soil from the hole.
- Fill the hole with water.
- Place the rose plant into the hole to the same depth it was in the pot, again being careful not to disturb the roots.
- Work the soil in around the root mass.
- Add about 2" to 3" of your favorite mulch. This helps hold soil moisture, keep the soil an even temperature and control weed growth.
- **Most important!** Water thoroughly and frequently, perhaps even daily for the first two weeks while the plant is adapting itself to its new home.
- After the plant is established, an average of 1/2" of water twice a week is sufficient. Most established roses can even exist quite well, thank you, on even less water. Roses are quite drought tolerant once they become established.
- Space the rose bushes six feet apart to allow for air circulation and efficient growth.

Good soil and water in an 18" diameter hole

Plant at the same depth it was growing in the pot

Mulch well & water frequently until established

Maintenance suggestions for your roses
- Walk through your rose garden every day. There are always discoveries to be made. Even if you spot a problem, it's small enough to solve with little effort. *Take time to smell the roses.*
- Proper watering will reduce stress and encourage healthy growth of roots, leaves and buds.
- Don't fertilize during dry spells unless you are watering.
- Avoid watering in the evening to prevent the development and spread of fungus diseases like Blackspot. Watering when the leaves are dry will also help to prevent the spread of fungus diseases.
- Use a quality encapsulated slow release fertilizer with minor elements. We recommend Osmocote or StaGreen Polyon because you only need to fertilize every six to twelve months with whatever fertilizer you choose.
- Fertilizer rule of thumb: Slow release fertilizers in the summer last only about half as long as stated on the package. This isn't really crucial because you can't really overfeed with a slow release fertilizer.
- Don't be afraid to cut bouquets of roses to share with others. You can brighten the day for a lot of people by simply sharing a flower.
- Prune to control growth, remove spent flowers and open the bush for good air circulation. When you prune, use sharp shears; it's a lot easier on your hands and much better for the plant.
- Do not use Roundup around roses. It's a sure killer. Even spray drift can send your favorite rose bush to the compost pile.

With just a little care roses will last years longer in the South than they do farther north. The proper varieties in the Fortuniana rootstock make a world of difference. Don't take my word for it. Just try it for yourself.

The red rose, born so full of promise fades a bit each day,
And life departs with each petal's fall.
Perhaps there's a lesson for us, these flowers have to say,
The gift of joy is given to us all.

PART ONE

Mulches for roses

- Pine Bark chips work well, have a good fragrance and last for some time before becoming compost, then humus.
- Cypress mulch is effective and has good fragrance, but we don't recommend it because of environmental problems.
- Eucalyptus, Meleleuca or Eco-Mulches are good, relatively long lasting and inexpensive. They are viable alternatives to cypress mulch.
- Sawdust is a cheap mulch but it tends to pack and slow water and air flow into the soil. Sawdust also contains little in the way of nutrients and can encourage some insects.
- Oak leaves and pine straw are natural, readily available and effective as mulches. Pine needles are long lasting and provide great air and water circulation. Pine straw is flammable, but insects aren't a serious problem. Leaves are nutrient rich and as they decompose into humus literally feed the roses.
- Groundcovers can be an effective living mulch that will help to control weeds, and do all the other things we want a mulch to do. Don't worry about the groundcover plants stealing food from the roses. Some groundcovers produce flowers that can detract from the rose display. Ivy, mondo grass, thyme, chocolate mint and chives all work well. The herbs also tend to discourage some of the insects.
- Fabric weed blocks and mats are also effective as long as they are porous and allow air and water to flow. Solid clear or black plastic should not be used. A light covering of other mulch or stone chips can be used over the landscape fabric for the sake of appearance.
- Stone chips, marble, scoria, crushed brick and others add no nutrients but are durable. Some can change the pH of the soil.
- Newspapers can be used but, because there is nothing quite as ugly as yesterday's news, they are best covered with a more attractive material. Newspaper can be shredded or used in full sheets. It does become humus and adds some nutrients to the soil. Don't apply it too many sheets thick or it can become a barrier to water and air.

IN THE ROSE GARDEN

Nipping problems in the bud: tips for rose growing
- Yellow leaves, or heavy leaf drop, generally indicate that a rose bush needs more water.
- Feast and Famine in nutrient levels can weaken a rose bush and make it more susceptible to fungus and insect attack. This is another reason why a slow release fertilizer is more efficient.
- Stem dieback is not a natural condition. It is usually a result of over-feeding, or heavy feeding and under watering.
- Growth from below the graft is the rootstock in rebellion, and this is natural and normal. This growth is best removed before it's vigor overtakes the rest of the plant. These are called suckers and can easily be removed by simply snapping them off.
- Be careful when applying household chemicals as homemade remedies. These can often do far more harm than good and aren't recommended in Florida's heat.
- When it's necessary to apply garden chemicals be careful to apply at the proper concentrations and with proper temperature and weather conditions.
- Weeds are best controlled with good old-fashioned human hands, but mulch also helps.

Hybrid tea rose

PART ONE

How to Kill a Rose

Murder most foul in the rose garden

There are multitudes of ways that diabolical gardeners can play the role of the Terminator in the rose garden. Let's look at a couple of profiles of these rose assassins.

The Prune & Feed Murderer

Characterized by a lot of nervous energy, frequently seen with heavy duty pruning shears and a large bag of rose food. The MO is something like this. On a beautiful Saturday morning this gardener slips into the rose beds and viciously attacks the plants with the shears. The once beautiful shrubs that might have become a bit leggy, are reduced to leafless stubble. Then the perpetrator will dump great handfuls of rose food on the soil around the victim who is already in shock. A slow and horrible death follows within days.

This is so important that we can't stress it enough. The surest way to kill a rose is to prune it, then immediately feed. When you have pruned the top growth you have destroyed the natural balance between the underground half of the plant and the stems, leaves and flowers that we see. Then plant foods are absorbed by the roots with limited places to put them in the rest of the plant. Fertilizer burn then occurs, with fatal consequences.

In the North roses were pruned back severely for the winter, then covered with mulch or insulating materials. Feeding occurred in the spring as new growth began and the soil was cool. Here in Florida our roses don't go dormant in the winter so that northern fall pruning isn't necessary.

Never prune at any time of the year below waist level, but you can prune at any time you like, except during a thunder storm. Pruning shears make a great lightening rod.

The Cozy Garden Murderer

This gardener lacks self confidence and subconsciously assumes that whatever he or she plants is going to fail to grow. The MO is to plant rose bushes literally inches apart and watch them grow together into one solid mass of leaves, twigs and stems. Because no air can circulate around these plants fungus diseases spread rapidly once they start. And the fact that the plants are crowded together means they are already weakened and suffering.

The problem is a lack of confidence on the part of the gardener. The faulty thinking is that either the roses aren't going to make it and we were only planting a bouquet, or, perhaps, these are bonsai roses that are never going to grow beyond the size they are in the container the day they were purchased.

Space the roses six feet apart and give them room to grow. Then prune occasionally to encourage air circulation.

The Feast & Famine Murderer

Often this is a case of negligent homicide involving liquid or fast release fertilizers as the murder weapon. The perpetrator feeds with a liquid snack food, then neglects to feed again for months. The rush of nutrients causes a quick flush of leaves but the plant then lacks the ability to sustain this tender new growth. Insects and fungi are more likely to attack the overfed, obese plant and general decline is often followed by death.

The safest way to feed roses in Florida is with an encapsulated slow release fertilizer like Osmocote or StaGreen Polyon.

With these timed-release fertilizers it's almost impossible to cause fertilizer burn by overfeeding, and the feast and famine cycle can be avoided.

Rambo in the Rose Garden

This rose assassin enters the garden like a commando on a raid, heavily armed with an arsenal of weapons designed to kill everything that crawls, creeps, hops or takes wing. The typical garden Rambo can read but doesn't, assuming reading the directions is an activity for weaklings and insecure wimps who don't understand that gardening is WAR. Typically these perpetrators use lawn and garden chemicals at far greater concentrations than recommended and applied with a maniacal blood lust that can lay waste the rose garden for generations to come, make the lawn unsafe for children

PART ONE

to play on and convert the backyard into an EPA declared toxic disaster zone.

Using the chemicals designed for our defense in ways that they weren't intended can kill the very plants they were designed to protect.

Read the directions carefully, then follow them, not triple the dosage just to be certain.

Using Roses in the Residential Landscape — Beyond the Rose Garden

One rose does a garden make, all else is trimming. Anon

We have been brought up to view roses as a thing of grace and beauty grown in specially designated rose gardens where they are grouped with others of their own kind. This kind of segregation is a traditional way of growing roses. The French, led by their great rosarians during the age of enlightenment planted and maintained great formal rose gardens, but even there, the roses were blended with green hedges, water features and other plants.

Creating a rose garden doesn't mean that you are limited to growing only roses in it, although they can be dramatic and dynamic when displayed in large groups. The rose walk at EPCOT and the rose garden at the Harry P. Leu Gardens in Orlando are prime examples of the beauty of mass plantings.

Often, however, the average homeowner doesn't have the space to devote to this type of rose garden and can only grow a few roses, perhaps only one or two. There are some opportunities for the homeowner that are often overlooked.

Roses can be grown along with other plants and shrubs, they don't have to be clustered together. In fact the spacing of roses among other plants can help to reduce the spread of fungus diseases and serious insect infestations. A rose bush or two certainly deserves a place in every herb garden, in a foundation planting, along a drive or walkway, as an accent for a fountain, around a gazebo, clambering over an arbor or fragrancing a favorite sitting area. The delightful fragrance of roses can add much to the average Florida room, serve as a flowering hedge, or become a protective security system planted under windows.

When we accent the roses with other plants such as the dwarf hollies, boxwood, groundcovers, herbs or other flowering shrubs we can create a mood in a small area, provide complimentary texture and contrasting colors while providing visual impact even when the roses are out of bloom, or not at their peak. There is such great diversity in the types, forms and varieties of roses available to Southern and Florida gardeners that you can set your imagination free and plant them throughout your landscape, anywhere that the color and fragrance will serve you well.

Remember, roses have a few basic needs that you can satisfy:
- A place in the sun for at least six hours a day
- A well drained location where they can put down roots
- A location where they can receive an average 1 inch of water per week, through irrigation or hand watering, if necessary.
- A location where you can maintain good air circulation
- Most important, a site where you can enjoy them

Some Ways to Use Roses in the Landscape
Old roses (or, if you prefer, antique, heritage or old-fashioned roses) and many of our modern carefree roses provide a lot of potential for the homeowner. These old roses are survivors, tough as nails and perfectly capable of taking care of themselves. They are the roses that can survive on their own with minimal attention from you. In fact, they can even be used for naturalizing or for massed plantings where pampering isn't a part of the overall landscape plan. These roses will withstand drought, heat, humidity, bugs, chainsaws and high taxes. See details on varieties in the Carefree section of the chapter called "Book of Lists" starting on page 22.

But there is a place for the modern roses, the hybrid teas, floribundas and even the miniatures in the home landscape.

Look at the advantages roses offer to the average suburban homestead.
- variety and diversity or color

- fragrance throughout a blooming season that lasts almost all year
- diversity in form and shape, from bush to climber or creeping groundcovers
  - roses can be either formal or informal
  - Good floral display during the snowbird season

Roses in the Border

We are so locked into the image of roses in the rose garden that we ignore their value as a border shrub. They are effective against a fence, or marking a boundary all on their own. Because of the growth habit of roses, particularly the shrub roses, and the fact that they usually have thorns (prickles for the purists) they are a natural at traffic control. Yet, the flowers soften the blow and project the image of a friendly neighbor.

These border or background roses can be mixed with other rose varieties, or with other plants, perennials or shrubs to create an attractive, active landscape feature. Roses are much more interesting than a chain link or cedar fence. You can vary the height, color, form or seasonal effect with some planning. These borders and boundaries can be in a straight line but often curves, waves or irregular lines can add interest and soften the effect.

The smallest of the shrub roses, and many of the miniatures, can be used as edgings where screening is undesirable or unnecessary. A walkway, drive or floral bed can be lined with these little charmers. Roses even make an effective foundation plant providing color and fragrance. There will be a need for sufficient sunlight and air circulation but, again, the old fashioned roses can come to the rescue.

Accenting Landscape and Hardscape Features

We think of the rose as the prima donna, unwilling to be anything but the center of attention, the focal point of the landscape. But, they also work extremely well as an accenting background for other feature plants and perennials. Shrub roses can be used to surround or frame fountains, birdbaths, gazing balls, even garden gnomes. They work well behind or beside a bench or garden seating area.

Not only do they serve as a background for flower border or bed, roses play well with evergreens like junipers, hollies and boxwood, even grass. A rose bush reflected in a water feature, behind a small pond or pool is beautiful and spiritually satisfying.

Roses in Decorative Containers

Yes, we do grow our roses in containers, but this is done to produce a healthy root system, provide convenience to the consumer and make planting easy and foolproof any time of the year. We don't grow our roses in containers with the intention that this be a permanent home.

Miniature roses are great as potted plants. Even some of the old shrub roses, polyanthas and floribundas will work well as container plants, but most of the roses that thrive in Florida with its extended growing season need more leg room for their roots than most containers provide. You can use any rose in a large container with proper drainage as a showcase plant for a season or two, but it will soon become rootbound and begin to show signs of stress. You can also go to the effort of giving your potted rose a root pruning annually. About one third of the root system will need to be trimmed away and new soil added. Having said this, there are some of our roses that will do very well in large or ornamental pots. Summer Snow and Pink Summer Snow will cascade over a container at will. Mother's Day, Europeana and Knockout also do reasonably well as potted plants.

Roses in Raised Beds

In soggy soils, areas where flooding can be a problem, or where the water table is close to the soil surface roses can be grown quite well in raised beds. These beds can range from 16 to 24 inches above the soil line and be made out of synthetic lumber, treated timbers, landscape stone, concrete block or your favorite material. I've been told that used tires work well. Regardless of the material, this structure can then be filled with reasonably good soil and roses planted as you would in the garden. This does give the advantage of easier access if you have a back problem or mobility limitations. If you use a raised bed that is between two and four feet wide this will make for easy maintenance. Any rose that will grow well in Florida

PART ONE

will grow well in Florida in a raised bed.

Value of climbers

We tend to overlook the climbing roses. This is unfortunate because they have so much potential. Think vertical. We can add a whole new dimension to the landscape. Climbers are often thought of as scraggly vines sprawling over an arbor or running rampant on an old abandoned fence row. But this vigorous growth habit makes climbing roses valuable trained on arbors, pergolas, gazebos, tripods, posts, pillars and fences of many types. They can even climb the side of a building if given some support.

Climbers can produce more flowers than the bush and shrub form roses because the more horizontal the cane, the more blooms will be produced. Roses tend to produce buds on terminal growth, but if the cane is trained along a fence, or the top of a pergola, flowers will appear at many of the leaf nodes.

Climbers use their prickles (thorns) to hold the canes in place when climbing over trees, fences, abandoned cars or other objects. However, for most situations where we will be growing climbing roses we will still need to secure the canes to their support using twist ties, slip-ties, cordage, or old nylon pantyhose. Note, experts suggest that it's best to use a figure 8 in the tie rather than simply strapping the stem to the support. This should help prevent damage to the canes.

There are several considerations to contemplate before rushing out to your nearest first class garden center to purchase a trunk full of Nelsons' climbing roses. Climbers need room to grow, often the canes will exceed 12 or 15 feet in length. When you train a climber on a wall, fence, gazebo, pergola or other architectural feature, chances are that at some point you will need to paint that structure. This may be a challenge if the roses are literally nailed to the wall. When roses are trained on the wall there is often insufficient air circulation and the potential for fungus attack increases, for both the roses and the building material.

One of the most effective ways to prevent future problems is to use the synthetic lumber made from recycled plastic products. It never needs painting and will last decades.

We think of climbers trained on fences, and this can be very attractive, but they also work well trained on tripods, posts or pillars. In fact, climbing roses that were somewhat more restrained were called pillar roses. Pillars can be made from the same synthetic lumber mentioned above, then the canes can be trained as a spiral, braid or weave around the post. Once the canes reach the top of the pillar the growth will flare into an umbrella like cascade that is striking. You can also use wires or wood to connect posts and the roses will grow across them to make a floral arch, or succession of arches.

Roses and Gardening for Nature
Many of the old shrub roses can be used as groundcovers because they will arch, creep and ramble. In many parts of the northern hemisphere roses naturally cover banks and hillsides where they help to prevent erosion, become a part nature's soil building process and provide cover and nesting sites for wildlife. The berries, or hips, also provide food for a multitude of birds and other wildlife.

Because these heritage roses are carefree, they can be used in areas where maintenance is difficult, feeding schedules impossible and erosion a real threat. Once established these old fashioned roses are quite capable of taking care of themselves and can become naturalized. They deserve consideration in the xeriscape garden because they are drought tolerant as well. There is a great diversity of form, color and blooming season to choose from.

Roses on Golf Courses and Commercial Landscaping

"If roses are as easy to grow as we say, then why aren't they found in commercial plantings more often?" is a question we are frequently asked. Let's look at the facts.

Many people have been programmed to think of roses as being labor intensive, because they require all that pruning, feeding and spraying. Yet they are easier to care for than most of the tropical plants we try to cultivate in commercial landscapes, and a rose garden isn't going to freeze out if we have a frost. Roses require far less care and maintenance than turf. In fact, grass is the most labor intensive plant we grow in Florida.

Others complain about the cost of roses compared to the cost of bedding plants, but again let's look at the facts. Roses are planted once and will last for five to ten years or more. Bedding plants have to be replaced three or four times a year. Incidently, bedding plants require more maintenance than roses, and are even more susceptible to insects and fungus disease. They are also subject to far greater damage from weather, drought, heat and cold.

Then why not more roses in commercial landscapes?

There are so many great, beautiful and rugged shrub roses that require little or no spraying and only occasional maintenance, that you would think that commercial landscapers would be planting roses everywhere, but this isn't the case.

This is partly due to a perception that dates back to the days before the Fortuniana rootstock, when roses were a far greater challenge in Florida than they are today. Old habits are hard to break.

Another factor is that many of the landscape designers draw up their plans calling for the use of what they are growing, and few of them grow roses.

For others it is the simple fact that they make a living from doing landscape maintenance and it is far more profitable for them to replace bedding annuals several times a year than it is to create long lived rose beds and borders.

Advantages for commercial sites

If you play golf on the Buena Vista course at Walt Disney World, you will find several plantings of some of our most rugged shrub roses growing there. As golf courses feel the pressure of a dwindling water supply we will see more and more of this, because these shrub roses are literally carefree and use far less water than many other traditional golf course plantings and far less maintenance and water than any of the grasses used.

The average rose bush will be in bloom about nine or ten months a year in Florida. This is why the theme parks plant so many roses, lots of color, fragrance and lasting beauty with no more than average maintenance. Wouldn't a bed of roses be more appealing than a

IN THE ROSE GARDEN

grouping of India hawthorn or azaleas that only bloom for a few weeks in the spring?

Wouldn't the tradition, the color and fragrance of roses be a valuable addition to the landscape of hospitals, doctor's offices, nursing homes, schools, office buildings, work places, even stores and shopping malls? Not only is there an aesthetic value to roses, there is a psychological benefit as well.

Carefree choices for commercial plantings

The following is a list of some of the most carefree roses that need little or no spraying with fungicides. These are ideal candidates for commercial and institutional planting.

Old garden roses
Louis Phillippe (Cracker Rose)
Duchesse de Brabant
Mrs. B. R. Cant
Old Blush
Clotilde Soupert
Carefree Beauty
Anna Oliver
Souvenir de la Malmaison

Modern shrub roses
Abraham Darby (David Austin)
Belinda's Dream
Bonica
Carefree Beauty
Carefree Wonder
China Doll
Heritage (David Austin)
Knockout
Margo Koster
Mothersday
Summer Snow
Pink Summer Snow
Sea Foam

See the listing of low maintenance roses on the next page for more roses ideal for commercial and institutional applications.

Gardens are not made by sitting in the shade.
                                        Rudyard Kipling

Part 2
Mark Nelson's Book of Lists

Carefree and Low Maintenance Roses

It is by believing in roses that one brings them to bloom.
French proverb

O. F. Nelson & Sons produces many thousands of roses every year. These roses are all winners in our careful selection process to determine the best growing varieties for Florida. We look at the color, fragrance, tolerance to heat, humidity and drought. We also look at longevity, growth habits, blooming cycles, overall ruggedness, versatility, adaptability and resistance to disease. Rare is the rose that scores high for us in all of these categories. Our goal is to produce the best roses available for the everyday gardener who happens to like roses and wants to enjoy them without pampering and special care. Here are my personal favorites.

Belinda's Dream. My all time favorite, is a beautiful pink shrub rose with a delightful, spicy, almost raspberry-like fragrance. This is a prolific ever-blooming rose producing full, double, high-centered flowers with an average of 40 petals or more on a fast growing bush that easily reaches six feet in height and, if given the freedom to do so, will become almost as wide. For those who are curious about where a new variety comes from, Belinda's Dream was developed and introduced in 1992 by Dr. Bayse in Caldwell, Texas. The parentage includes Tiffany and Jersey Beauty. It was named for the daughter of a friend. It was selected at the EPCOT Flower &

PART 2

Garden Festival as the Perfect Florida Rose! It has also been the first rose selected as a "Special Texas Rose."

Why Belinda's Dream is at the top of my list:
- It's at home in any rose garden. It plays well with other roses.
- It's a dramatic specimen landscape plant and can stand all alone as a focal point. If you were only going to grow one rose this would be it.
- It's everblooming and makes an excellent cut flower.
- It's best pruned by cutting bouquets to share with friends, neighbors and total strangers, or to be enjoyed by yourself.
- Because of the crisp color and rich fragrance it ought to be planted around doctors' offices, hospitals, nursing homes and business sites.
- It's heat tolerant and cold hardy, eager to please throughout Florida and far beyond this state's borders.
- It's disease resistant and needs no spraying or special care.
- This is a truly carefree rose.

> *Earth laughs in flowers.*
> Ralph Waldo Emerson

Top Carefree Roses for Florida
Carefree roses are simply roses that require no spraying or special care beyond what you give to the landscape in general. In fact, the carefree roses mentioned below are less demanding than many of the commonly used landscape shrubs, bedding plants and exotics that are so popular with our landscape architects and designers.

On occasion I have referred to carefree roses as "weed roses" and there is some truth to this. A weed grows without constant primping and doesn't whimper at the sight of every bug that crawls across a petal. In the past many of the carefree roses were once bloomers, or offered small, poorly colored flowers. However, today's ever-expanding list of carefree roses has a lot to offer. They require less pruning than podocarpus or ligustrum, more color than India hawthorns, and a blooming season that doesn't stop like azaleas. Hibiscus require far more maintenance than our carefree roses and a cold snap isn't nearly the threat to roses that it is to those hibiscus.

> **Note:** Carefree roses are the ideal landscape plant for snowbirds and seasonal residents in Florida because they will give color and fragrance throughout the winter months and survive neglect through the summer with a good mulch and a feeding with a timed-release fertilizer.

Most of our Carefree roses are classified as shrub roses and further listed as either *Old Garden Roses* or *Modern Shrub Roses*.

Old Garden Roses

These have a special charm because they are survivors and whisper to us in their forms, colors and fragrances of our own human history. The mystique of the rose is linked with the mystique of our own story.

Anna Oliver produces large full rich pink blossoms continuously on a vigorous but not sprawling bush. The flowers are also quite fragrant. It was first introduced in France in 1872. Can be grown in a container, but is most effective in group plantings or as a rose border.

Carefree Beauty is a repeat bloomer that produces large medium pink flowers with a fruity fragrance. The petals tend to lighten with age. This hardy and rugged rose was developed in the United States and introduced in 1977.

Carefree Wonder is another pink shrub rose with pale, cream to pink blossoms. The semi-double flowers are large and lightly fragrant. Carefree Wonder has a bushy growth habit and is a profuse repeat bloomer that will give color almost all year long. This is a great rose for hedges, borders and mass plantings. It was developed in France and introduced in 1990.

Clotilde Soupert produces full white, or blended white, flowers with a rich fragrance. This is a polyantha rose introduced to the public in 1890.

Duchesse de Brabant has globe shaped, light, almost frosted pink flowers with a pronounced fragrance. This is one of those early French introductions (1857) whose parentage is a mystery. This classic rose has an alias or two to further confuse matters. It's also known

PART 2

as Contessa de Labarthe and Contessa Bertha.

Louis Phillippe is the classic Carefree rose for Florida. It is one of the easiest and most dependable roses you can grow. This rich red, recurrent flowering rose is sometimes sold as the "Cracker Rose." It is listed as a China and a Bourbon rose and dates back to 1834.

Old Blush has semi-double medium pink flowers and is a dependable almost constant bloomer. This was the first China rose introduced to Europe and that event took place in the 1780s. This was the first exposure of the Europeans to a repeat blooming rose. It has been used in the breeding of many of our modern roses. It's also known as Parson's Pink monthly, Pink Monthly and Old Pink Daily rose.

Mrs. B. R. Cant gives you a continuous display of globe-shaped blended pink double flowers on a compact bush that is noted for its disease resistance. Color is variable depending on temperatures. The fragrance is refreshing but not overpowering. This tea rose was developed in England and introduced in 1901. It was named by the hybridizer, Benjamin Cant, for his wife.

Souvenir de la Malmaison produces a multitude of soft, light pink, full double blossoms with 65 to 75 petals. It has a pleasant spicy fragrance. This dependable repeat blooming Bourbon rose was introduced in 1843 in Beluze, France. It was named in honor of the Empress Josephine's fabulous rose garden at her chateau Malmaison near Versailles. The name, Malmaison, means house of death, so named because it was a former leper colony. Josephine lived at Malmaison from 1799 until her death in 1814. It was while living on this estate that she pursued her gardening with a passion.

Carefree Modern Shrub Roses

These roses expand on the themes of disease resistance and rugged life style as they provide more colors, greater variety in flower form and a diversity of growth habits than the old shrub roses. The following are the modern shrub roses we have found to be the most dependable. Several of these are described as David Austin roses. This is an English rose breeder and grower who has done much work in developing roses for everyday people. While many of the David Austin roses don't adapt well to our Florida climate, some are a valuable and dependable addition to our rose gardens.

Abraham Darby (pat # 7215) is a David Austin rose with an antique rose look and thoroughly modern parents. The flowers are large and full with a delightful blend of pink suffused to apricot. This dependable repeat bloomer was named after one of the pioneers of the industrial revolution

Belinda's Dream, a rose so perfect that it has a page all of its own. See page 23. It is also on the front cover of this book.

Bonica, what a beautiful scarlet floribunda rose this is. The medium size flowers may have as many as 70 petals and form on large sprays with a delicate rose scent. This is a vigorous bush that will grow with enthusiasm and bloom repeatedly throughout the year. It was developed in France by the Meillands and was introduced in 1958.

China Doll is a floribunda with masses of diminutive vivid pink or fuchsia flowers in full clusters. There is a light rose scent with the flowers but it isn't as rich as many other polyanthas. This is a compact and bushy plant that works well in beds, as a border planting and even as a container rose. It was developed in the United States and introduced in 1946.

Heritage is a David Austin rose with a clear, soft pink center that fades to almost white in the outer petals of the medium sized full bloom. The fragrance is rich with an almost sweet, honey-like hint.

Iceberg is a dramatic white rose that is in most rosarian's list of favorites. It has, for more than forty years, been the standard against which many other roses were measured. This floribunda was released in 1958 ans is in the parentage of many of the David Austin roses. The classic white, double, hauntingly fragrant blooms are produced profusely most of the year. It is also tough, resistant to insects, disease, drought and neglect. It's a great rose for bedding.

Knockout is a new rose with that fascinating Cherry-Popsicle red color. It was an All American Rose Selection in 2000. The single to semi-double flowers are produced non-stop and the fragrance is rich and delightful. It has great resistance to disease, insects and is quite drought tolerant. This is a rose with a great future as a bedding and landscape shrub.

Margo Koster is a floribunda that produces clusters of small,

PART 2

red-coral-orange blossoms with a light, spicy fragrance. Because it's a compact rugged, almost thornless bush, it is a good rose for containers, borders, walkways and mass plantings. This rose is a sport of Dick Koster, introduced in the Netherlands in 1931.

Mothers Day is a floribunda with carnation red flowers, small and globe shaped with a faint fragrance. This is a compact plant that will produce bright clusters of blooms throughout the year, making it an ideal subject for borders, walkways, bed, containers, or anywhere else that a rugged rose is needed. Mothers Day is another Dutch discovery and another sport of Dick Koster. It was introduced in 1949.

Pink Summer Snow is a floribunda that produces clusters of soft pink and white flowers with a light fragrance. The individual flowers are medium in size with an average of 25 petals. This is a disease resistant rose that will give continuous bloom and is ideal for beds, borders and mass plantings.

Sea Foam is a shrub rose that willingly gives you clusters of small, double, cream colored flowers on sprawling canes that can reach twelve feet in length. This is a repeat bloomer that isn't noted for fragrance. Because Sea Foam is such a vigorous plant, it is sometimes used as a groundcover, but it can be trained as a climber, on a fence or as a hedge. This was a U.S. introduction in 1964.

Sunflare (pat #5001) is a floribunda with medium yellow double blooms that open flat. These almost licorice-scented flowers are borne in clusters on short stems. It is a heavy bloomer with great disease resistance. It is a U.S. introduction from 1981.

Low-Maintenance Roses

Carefree roses are great, but there are many roses that are almost as easy. For simplicity we call these Low-Maintenance Roses. Among these are hybrid teas, floribundas, and even some climbers. These low-maintenance varieties will require a bit more care, but still far less than most folks think a rose demands. The advantages to growing these roses in the landscape include:
- At least 9 months of bloom a year
- No need to replant 2 to 4 times a year as you do annuals and bedding plants
- Minimal spraying, often no spraying is required at all

- Little concern for cold damage as there is with tropicals like hibiscus
- Only require feeding two or three times a year. These roses will perform well even with neglect.

Hybrid tea bloom

Low Maintenance Hybrid Tea Roses to Consider

Elina gives you large, dramatic ivory-yellow flowers in the classic hybrid tea form. The flowers on this reliable bloomer are lightly scented. It was developed in Ireland and introduced to the world in 1983. It's also known as *Peaudouce*, "soft skin," a reference to the velvety petals. This is the best of the low maintenance hybrid teas and has been called Belinda's Dream in a different color.

Granada is a beautiful multi color hybrid tea blending red, pink and yellow. Color intensity may change with the weather. Deeper shades prevail during the cool season. The flowers last well as a cut flower. It is also an extremely fragrant, spicy scented rose, receiving the Gamble Award for Fragrance in 1968. The bush ranges from 3 to 5 feet with good foliage. Granada is also known as Donatella. This is an American introduction from 1963.

Kentucky Derby produces good sized fragrant dark red blos-

PART 2

soms. Kentucky Derby is a dependable bloomer developed in the U.S. and released in 1972. It is a superb red rose.

Magic Lantern is listed as both a grandiflora and a hybrid tea. Either way you get a repeat blooming bush with enormous coppery-yellow-pink blended flowers. This rose was introduced in 1989 as a sport of Gold Medal. It is another upright growing bush that thrives throughout Florida, handling our heat quite well.

Montezuma produces double, high-centered blooms in a unique salmon-orange color. The fragrance is light but Montezuma is a dependable repeat bloomer. This U.S. developed rose was introduced in 1955.

Summer Dream (pat # 5640) dependably produces beautiful shell pink blossoms. The flower has good form to best show the soft color and light fragrance.

Gold Medal is a grandiflora well worth considering as a valuable addition to your landscape. Rich, deep, golden yellow flowers with a rich fragrance grace this 4 to 6 foot bush. It's disease resistant and heat tolerant.

St. Patrick was introduced in the U.S.A. in 1996 by Frank Strickland. It is an ideal clear yellow rose with a cool chartreuse

Floribunda rose

tinge. The growth habit is robust with the large double flowers held on long stems. This is an ideal yellow rose for all of Florida because it can take our heat.

Low-Maintenance Floribunda Roses to Consider

Brass Band (pat #9171) produces large apricot and yellow flowers with ruffled petals. This is a solid repeat blooming floribunda that does well in Florida with little care. The flowers are lightly fragrant, reminiscent of a Damask rose. Brass Band was developed in the United States and introduced in 1995.

Bridal Pink is another of the low-maintenance floribundas that does so well here. The flowers are light pink, large and high centered and produced in profusion. They have a distinctive mild, spicy fragrance and make excellent cut flowers. Bridal Pink was developed in the United States and introduced in 1967.

Charisma is a striking orange-red floribunda, so warm and cheery in color that it's bound to lighten your spirits. The medium size flowers are produced in clusters on an almost continuous basis. The fragrance is light and fruity. Charisma, also known as Surprise Party, was introduced in 1977.

Europeana produces clusters of rich crimson-red flowers that are double and open almost flat. Not only does it bloom almost all year long, the blossoms have a classic tea rose fragrance. This rose was developed in the Netherlands and introduced in 1963.

First Edition has a unique salmon-coral color and a pleasant light fragrance. This is a floribunda from the Delbards of France and was introduced in 1976. It is also known as the Arnaud Delbard.

Knockout is a new rose with that fascinating Cherry-Popsicle red color. It was an All American Rose Selection in 2000. The single to semi-double flowers are produced non-stop and the fragrance is rich and delightful. It has great resistance to disease, insects and is quite drought tolerant. It is the best and the easiest of the low maintenance floribundas.

Scentimental flowers are large and playful, red and white splashed, and they are produced in great quantities. The fragrance is as dramatic as the coloration, being heavy, spicy and sweet. Scentimental is a great rose for close viewing as a focal point, or a part of a border or rose garden. It was introduced in the U.S. in

PART 2

1997. It is a dependable repeat bloomer with a compact growth habit and rich deep green foliage.

Low Maintenance Climbing Roses for Florida
  Blossomtime blooms most of the year, producing a profusion of crisp medium pink flowers with forty petals or more. The fragrance is pronounced but not overpowering. This vigorous climber was introduced in 1951.
  Catherine Nelson is a climber producing quality rich pink flowers with a rich fragrance. The growth habit and floral form are like a Don Juan. It was developed by the Nelsons from a sport of Don Juan, and is named in honor of my mother.
  Don Juan is one of the most popular roses in Florida and it is the most widely grown red climber in the state. Who can resist those dramatic, crimson-red blossoms and the delightful fruity-citrus fragrance? It's even a great rose for cutting because the velvet petaled flowers are produced on long stems. It provides continuous bloom. It was developed in Italy from a cross on a New Dawn seedling and New Yorker. It was introduced in 1958.
  Spectra blossoms are a beautiful yellow-orange blend, large and lightly fragrant. This is a climber that doesn't ramble quite as vigorously as does the Don Juan or some of the other climbers. It comes to us from Meilland of France, and was introduced in 1983.
  Pinata is a heavy bloomer with full yellow blossoms tinted with oranges and red. Pinata is a rambling shrub that can easily be trained as a climber. It does well on a fence, against a wall, on a trellis or arbor. Pinata is almost everblooming and lightly fragrant.
  Prosperity produces large, fully double light pink or blush white blossoms with a delightful musk rose scent. This is a shrub rose that can easily be trained as a climber. It does well on a fence or trellis and can be used as an informal hedge. It is disease resistant, tolerates some shade and drought. Prosperity is an English introduction dating back to 1919. It is the best and easiest of the climbers to grow.
  Royal Gold is a climber that produces large rich yellow blossoms that possess a fruity fragrance singly or in small clusters. These relatively long stemmed flowers are great for cutting. Royal Gold isn't an overly vigorous climber but it can be trained on a fence,

trellis or other hardscape feature.

Sea Foam is a sprawling rose with small fully double flowers in clusters. The color is described as white, cream or pale blush. It is a dependable repeat bloomer with a light fragrance. This is a 1964 Conrad-Pyle introduction resulting from a cross with White Dawn and Pinocchio. Sea Foam is a rugged, disease resistant rose that can be used as a groundcover, trimmed to become an informal hedge or trained on fence, trellis or arbor.

Bonica is a red/scarlet flowered floribunda type rose with enough vigor to be considered a climber. The blossoms are produced in sprays with each flower containing 50 to 70 petals. The fragrance is mild and distinctly fruity. This rugged rose was introduced in France by the Meillands in 1958.

Tips on growing climbers:

Climbers are often overlooked when we plan for our rose gardens and home plantings. This is unfortunate because they have so much to offer. Most climbers are rugged. They can be used on a fence or wall, trained on a trellis, arbor, pillar, pergola, gazebo, used as a screen, background, security and groundcover. The following are some tips for using climbing roses in your landscape.

- Climbers can be trained on a post and rail fence, chain link fence or masonry wall to soften the stark image of the structure. Most varieties will provide color and fragrance with little care.
- Use supports that are heavy enough to carry the weight of a mature climbing rose. The synthetic lumber products now available don't even need painting and will last for years.
- Planting two climbers together gives more fullness and shape at the bottom.
- Planting two varieties together, such as a shrub rose and a climber will give great growth pattern, casual height, dramatic bloom and better all around shape. The following are a few combinations that work well together.

   Bonica/Blossomtime
   Love's Promise / Don Juan / Europeana
   Summer Snow, or Pink Summer Snow / Prosperity
   Pinata / Spectra

PART 2

Sea Foam / Prosperity
Belinda's Dream / Blossomtime

Top Fragrant Roses for Florida

Not all roses smell like we all think a rose is supposed to smell. One of the complaints voiced most often about florist type roses is that they don't have a fragrance. It's unfortunate that the cut flower industry chose to breed its roses for long stems and tight buds rather than the distinctive rose scents. Even the breeders of our modern roses have been forced to sacrifice some fragrance to get the dramatic color, form and foliage. The good news is that we still have a great selection of fragrant roses to chose from.

In recent years we have begun to take seriously the physical and psychological effects of fragrances, scents and aromas. This is often a part of serious recovery programs for stroke patients and can provide stimulation for Alzheimer's patients. Fragrance can even be used as a part of a treatment program for depression, grief recovery, stress reduction, drug and alcohol abuse and recover from surgery. The subject of aromatherapy is now being taken seriously as a way to stimulate the mind, relax the body, promote calmness and reduce stress. Perhaps some day the psychologist's couch will be replaced with a stroll through a rose garden and every doctor's waiting room will have a bouquet of roses in it.

Not all roses smell the same. Some produce a fruity, apple or berry scent. Others have a spicy, cinnamon, nutmeg or clove fragrance, while others give us the sweet, delicate aroma with musky overtones that are often referred to as the typical rose scent. The James Alexander Gable Fragrance Award is given to roses that satisfy rigid demands of scent.

Here are some of my favorite fragrant roses.

Belinda's Dream	Granada	Tiffany
Chrysler Imperial	Mr. Lincoln	
Double Delight	Perfume Delight	
Flo Nelson	Regatta	
Scentimental	Saint Patrick	

My Favorites by Color

Red Roses
Kentucky Derby
Europeana
Don Juan (climber)
Mr. Lincoln
Chrysler Imperial

White Roses
Iceberg

Clothilde Soupert
Iceberg
Elina
Prosperity

Orange Roses
Tropicana
Brass Band
Cary Grant

Best Lavender
Angel Face
Paradise
Lagerfeld

Pink Roses
Belinda's Dream
McCartney
Regatta (a new Peachy-pink-coral)

Yellow Roses
Saint Patrick
Sun Flare
Gold Medal

Apricot
Summer Kiss
Sunset Celebration

Blends
Double Delight
Granada
Scentimental
Tiffany

Loveliest of lovely things are they,
On Earth, that soonest pass away.
The rose that lives its little hour
Is prized beyond the sculptured flower.
                    William Cullen Bryant

PART 2

Frequently Asked Questions

Here are some questions that the folks at Nelson's Roses are most often asked. I know that some of these provide the answers to questions you have as well.

What is your favorite rose?
I have three favorites. Belinda's Dream, because it's carefree, a heavy repeat bloomer, is the favorite all-around rose. I also have two sentimental favorites that were developed here. The Catherine Nelson is a pink climbing rose named for my mother. Flo Nelson was named in honor of my aunt.

Why are roses are grafted onto rootstocks?
Grafting is used as the primary means of rose propagation for several reasons. First, it gives a reliable reproduction of the original plant.
Second, it is the quickest way for the grower to grow a marketable rose bush. Third is the fact that roses grown on their own root often can't handle Florida's soils, climate and nematodes as well as the Fortuniana rootstock that we use.

How do you select the varieties you grow?
We work with rose hybridizers, constantly trial the new AARS winners and we study catalogs and lists for new colors and types of roses.

What is your selection criteria?
We graft these new roses onto Fortuniana rootstock, then evaluate them through the Florida summer. We look for varieties that repeat bloom and hold their color. We base our final decision on popularity, overall vigor and performance in our summer heat.

What is the most serious flaw a rose can have in your selection process?
I refuse to grow roses without roses. A rose bush or vine without flowers is not a rose. We don't consider roses foliage plants.

What are David Austin roses?
This is a series of fine roses introduced by the English rose grower, David Austin. His goal was to combine the best traits of the rugged, classic, old fashioned roses with the dynamics and beauty of modern varieties. What was produced was a number of varieties that had the form and fragrance of a historic rose and the repeat blooming tendencies of today's best. Not all David Austin roses perform well in Florida, but Abraham Darby and Heritage are excellent choices.

What are Dream roses?
This is a series of roses that has been well marketed and may be great in many parts of the country, but, generally they don't do well in Florida. The list of Carefree Roses from Nelsons' are proven survivors of the climate found in the Deep South. Our conditions are different and this means we have to have different solutions.

Why do roses cost so much?
A. They don't. If you look at the big picture, roses are a real bargain. Think of this as a math problem. To get as much color over as extended a period you have to plant annual bedding plants. How many annuals does it take to equal one rose bush? On average it would take eight to twelve annuals to give the color display of one rose bush. A quality rose may cost between $12 and $15. The annuals cost between 89 cents and $3.97. A rose bush will last for years while the annuals are actually "seasonals" in Florida and will need to be replaced three or four times each year. If the rose served your landscape for only five years that is an average of less than $3 per year. The annuals would cost you between $8 and $30 each year. Total cost in five years for the rose would be $12 to $15. For the bedding plants it would be between $40 and $150. The roses also require less maintenance, water and labor than the annuals. You decide which is the real bargain.

What is the average life span of a rose in Florida?
Roses in Florida will have an effective landscape life span that ranges from five to twenty years or more, if they are on the Fortuniana rootstock. This will vary with the care you give them

and the type of rose. Many of the shrub roses will last for generations and others will grow and bloom for decades.

I've heard that Black Spot is the biggest problem roses have in Florida. How serious is Black Spot?
Roses are not naturally heat tolerant. The stress from heat is a great deal of the problem with Black Spot. Most people tend to over react to this fungus problem. While it's true that it can't be controlled, and can only sometimes be prevented, it usually isn't a fatal disease. Most roses will recover quickly.

How far back should I prune my roses if they get Black Spot?
About 1 inch overall. This way you will feel that you have done something, and the bush will flush out. Of course, it will flush out whether you prune or not. Roses in Florida should not be pruned back lower than waist height because we don't have a winter dormancy period here.

Should I give my roses an extra feeding if they get Black Spot?
No. This will encourage tender new growth, a delicacy for the Black Spot. If you feel you must do something, give them a side dressing of Milorganite or Black Kow. These are safe slow release organic fertilizers.

What is a nematode?
Nematodes are sub-microscopic critters that abound in soil. Most are beneficial, but some attack the roots of your favorite plants and cause cancer-like growths where they literally suck the vitality from the plant. Over a period of time this weakens and eventually kills the plant. The Fortuniana root stock is resistant to nematode attack. Working lots of organic material into the soil before planting also helps to encourage the fungi and other organisms that dine on nematodes.

Why do some roses smell and others don't?
We always blame the rose breeders for the lack of fragrance in some roses, but the truth is that some of the old shrub roses didn't have any scent either. Most of the newer roses are bred with fra-

grance as one of the prime considerations. Roses also come with a wide range of scents including musk, spicy, fruity and traditional

Why are rose flowers smaller in the summer than in the cooler months?
A lot of the problem is simple heat stress that can affect both the size and the color of the blossoms. Another factor is the higher the temperature the faster the buds form. This can mean fewer petals, smaller petals and fewer flowers.

Is South Florida too tropical to grow roses?
Not at all. There are many excellent roses that will grow in Miami, the Keys, and Puerto Rico. Many beautiful roses can be found in the Bahamas, Cayman Islands, Jamaica, Costa Rica and much of the rest of the Caribbean basin.

Are roses salt tolerant?
Roses, generally, will thrive anywhere hibiscus will grow. This can vary with the variety, some being more tolerant than others. The Fortuniana rootstock also seems to be somewhat more salt tolerant than some of the others.

Can you grow roses in containers?
Yes and no. Most roses will grow quite well in raised beds. Many will grow in large containers with good drainage, but many of our larger growing roses need more root room than the average container provides. Having said that, there are miniatures and many of the smaller shrub roses that grow quite well in a large flower pot.

Can I grow roses in the shade?
Not very well. Actually, this depends on how dense the shade is. If the bush is going to get at least six hours of sun each day, then it will probably grow reasonably well. Most roses do much better in full sun, will bloom more and have fewer fungus problems. Louis Phillippe and many of the polyanthas will grow with some success in light shade.

What soil types work best for Florida roses?

PART 2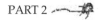

Roses, like most plants will grow better in better quality soil. That is, soil with lots of organic material, a good balance of nutrients and a pH that isn't too extreme. They will tolerate quite a bit less and still perform well. Roses do like a well drained soil and protest soil that remains soggy for more than a couple days.

How should I water my roses?

Roses are best watered in the morning. Drip irrigation is the most efficient way to water. Roses will do well with ½ inch of water twice a week. A good surface mulch helps to preserve soil moisture and keep the soil cooler.

Should roses be grown in exclusive rose gardens?

This is your decision. They don't have to be isolated and actually make good neighbors for many other plants. They can be used as a hedge, edging, accent or background plant in a flower bed or perennial border. Be creative and use roses everywhere. By spreading them out you can actually prevent many of the fungus and insect problems that can affect roses.

What about companion planting? Are there other plants that grow well with roses?

Use your imagination. It is your garden, your yard, your homestead. Roses and many of the herbs like rosemary, thyme, mints and chives do well together.

How should I feed my roses?

Using a slow release encapsulated plant food like Osmocote or Sta-Green Polyon every three to six months is the easiest and safest way to feed. This will give you stronger plants and there is no chance of fertilizer burn.

When Should I prune my roses?

After the rose has been in your landscape for a year. We give roses a good annual pruning about St. Valentine's Day, sometimes down to knee level, but no lower. During the rest of the year light maintenance pruning may be done, such as the removal of growth below the graft, or an errant cane, and, of course, deadheading.

Generally, don't prune lower than waist high for best results.

Do you have any pruning do's and don'ts?
Never prune below 24 inches. It's always better to prune too little than too hard. Roses can be pruned about waist high to promote more leaves, more blooms and a more attractive bush.

Never prune back hard in the fall. Only prune waist high and don't fertilize with any dry fertilizer immediately before or after pruning.

Remember that the new growth is going to come from the leaf nearest the pruning cut. This can cause growth toward the inside of the bush or cause it to bush out and be more open.

How do I prune my climbing roses?
Climbing roses can be pruned just like regular roses, with the same do's and don'ts. However, main canes that are left can be as long as you like. Pruning tells the bush to send out fresh leaves and flower buds.

What winter care is required for roses in Florida?
Winter is a season to enjoy roses at their best in Florida. They will bloom well here if kept watered. In the winter in Florida the rose blossom can be larger and the colors more intense because the bud develops more slowly. This is a great season to relax and smell the roses.

When is the best time to plant roses?
In the fall so that you can take full advantage of the heavier and fuller bloom that occurs during the cooler months.

What is the worst time to plant a rose bush?
Fourth of July. We are going into the stress season and the bush has to race to get established. Also, for many rose varieties, flowering is not prime in the hot months.

What season do you sell the most roses?
Mother's Day.

PART 2

Are there roses that will do well in our summer heat?
YES! The big three for summer bloom are Kentucky Derby, a beautiful and fragrant red rose, St. Patrick, a beautiful cool yellow, and Belinda's Dream, vivid pink color and a spicy fragrance.

Can't I plant roses anytime?
Yes, container roses can be planted anytime it isn't raining. If you plant them while it's raining you'll get all wet.

Should I purchase a rose with flowers on it?
By all means. This is the way you can tell what you're buying. This is one of the advantages of purchasing container grown stock.

After planting the new rose bush should I trim off all the buds?
Not unless you have some irresistible urge to see only green leaves. Let the buds become flowers, after all that's what you bought the plant for in the first place.

What's the biggest mistake people make when they plant roses?
There are three big mistakes people make when they are growing roses.

1. Planting them too close together. I guess most of us don't expect our plants to grow up.

2. Over-feeding and under-watering. This kills more roses than anything else you can do to them.

3. Fussing and worrying about them so much that you don't take time to enjoy them.

Roses, American as Apple Pie (a Quiz)

The rose has been called the universal flower, embraced and cultivated by all peoples, but there are some uniquely American connections to the rose as well. The fact is that there was an American love affair with the rose long before there was an America. Through the years this connection has been formalized and institutionalized. Roses are as American as apple pie. Let's see how well you do with this little quiz.

1. The rose is the official floral symbol of the United States of America since which of our presidents signed it into law?
(A) Dwight David Eisenhower, (B) Ronald Reagan, (C) Jimmy Carter, (D) Harry S. Truman.

2. The rose was determined to be the favorite flower of America in a series of public opinion polls. The percentage of people who favored the rose was
(A) 60%, (B) 75%, (C) 85%, (D) 95%

3. The rose is the official flower of the District of Columbia, but it is also the state flower of how many states?
(A) 2, (B) 3, (C) 4, (D) 5, (E) 7

4. What month is National Rose Month in the United States?
(A) June, (B) May, (C) February, (D) November

5. Who established the White House Rose Garden?
(A) Martha Washington, (B) Abigail Adams, (C) Eleanor Roosevelt, (D) Mrs. Ellen Wilson

PART 2

Answers to: Roses, as American as Apple Pie

1. (B) Ronald Reagan signed the act into law on Nov. 20th, 1986.
2. (C) 85% of the Americans polled preferred the rose.
3. (C) four states have roses as their official state flower: Georgia, Iowa, New York and North Dakota.
4. (A) June
5. (D) Woodrow Wilson's first wife, Ellen, was an avid gardener who was responsible for the rose garden as we know it today.

Part 3
Beyond the Rose Garden

Using Roses as Cut Flowers

Part of the allure of roses is that we can do things with them. Rose gardens are active, not passive. I don't mean the labor, even if it is a labor of love, that we think we have to invest in the cultivation of these charmers. I'm referring to the fact that, unlike hibiscus, roses make excellent cut flowers. In fact they are by far the most popular cut flowers in the world. Even a rose weak on fragrance has more scent than most orchids. Roses throughout history have been used, not just enjoyed. While we view a beautiful rose as a work of art, it is also a workhorse. Roses have been valued as herbs for both medicinal and culinary use. They have been used to brighten the dull, dark and dank rooms of the castles of kings and queens, but they have also been the flower of choice of the everyday people. Part of this love affair with the rose is because it is the perfect cut flower.

There are so many directions, professional secrets , secret formulas, and folk tales about the ways we are supposed to cut and prepare roses for floral bouquets that the average rose gardener gets confused, discouraged or paranoid. The following is the way many florists suggest that you do it.

• Some sources say morning is the best time to cut roses for bouquets, other sources recommend late afternoon. In Florida morning works better, because of the possibility of heat stress in the afternoon. Some suggest cutting while there is still dew on the flowers, others tell us to wait until the dew has disappeared. The real

PART THREE

it's the right time."
- Roses that have been watered a couple hours before cutting are better hydrated and tend to last longer.
- Select buds that are about halfway open. Flowers that aren't fully open will give you longer vase life. Buds that are too tight, without give or spring when gently squeezed, probably will not open.
- Carry a glass of cool water with you if possible. The less time the stems are out of water the less deterioration to the flowers.
- Make a clean cut on the stem at a 45 degree angle, about one-half inch above a leaf.
- Allow yourself enough stem to be able to make a fresh cut when arranging the blossoms later.
- Think of the harvesting of flowers for bouquets as a way to prune the bush. This is also a good time to be on the lookout for other pruning that needs to be done, insect damage, mulch replacement, watering and other elements of routine maintenance.
- As soon as possible get the cut roses inside. Refrigerate them if you aren't going to be working with them immediately.
- When doing the arranging make a fresh cut on the stem, again using sharp shears. Some florists suggest doing this under cold running water, but the important thing is to get the stem back in the water as soon as possible.
- It isn't necessary to smash, pound with a hammer or chew on the end of the stems. A good clean cut will suffice.
- Don't add salt, aspirin, cinnamon or any other secret formula to the water. The key to prolonging the life of the bouquet is to change the water frequently and keep the container out of the direct sun.

It may well be that the secret isn't in how we harvest the blooms, prepare the stems and display them, but rather how we share them. Roses have the power to make people smile. When a rose is given to friend or stranger it speaks more clearly than any words, in any language, "You have a friend. Someone cares about your existence."

Your life is enriched when you bring your roses into your home where you can enjoy them at any time of the day, in any weather. But your life can be even more enriched by sharing the beauty of your rose garden with the nurses in a hospital, nursing home residents, a lonely neighbor or teacher. Barriers of age, culture, language, faith, occupation, education and lifestyle all melt into oblivion when a rose is shared. Try it. The rose is one of God's great gifts to us. It's only right that we share the gift.

> No matter how or when you cut your roses, refrigerate them

> 'Tis the last rose of summer,
> Left blooming alone;
> All her lovely companions
> are faded and gone.
> Thomas Moore

> *Gather ye rosebuds while ye may. Olde time is still a-flying,*
> *And this same flower that smiles today, Tomorrow will be a dying.*
> Robert Herrick

Roses Can Be Dried

Gather ye rosebuds while ye may. Olde time is still a-flying,
And this same flower that smiles today, Tomorrow will be a-dying.
Robert Herrick

Roses given and received on special occasions or roses that have significance can be photographed, but often we need a more dimensional memory. Roses can be dried, but they will change colors, usually darkening or browning. They also will become somewhat brittle unless they are soaked in a glycerine-water mixture for a day or two before the drying process begins. Here are some of the most popular ways to dry roses. Visit your library for entire books on the art of flower drying.

- The simplest way to dry roses is hang the flowers upside down in a room where they will be out of the sun, but still have good air circulation. To help hold the petals in the bloom they can be sprayed with an aerosol hair spray or a clear craft finish. The drying process can take from a couple days to over a week to com-

PART THREE

plete. If the flowers have begun to droop on the stem before you started the drying process hanging upside down will usually cause them to straighten out again, but you can use a piece of florist wire is you wish.

- Rose petals and flowers can also be dried in a microwave oven if they have short stems. This works best with a microwave that has a turntable. Place on paper towels and turn every minute or so to prevent toasting. Please note that you must use a low setting to dry flowers properly in a microwave.
- Silica gel and Borax remain reliable ways to effectively dry roses. It is important to fully cover the flower and get some of the desiccant into and around the petal cluster. Drying with this method can take a week or more but can give the best color preservation.
- In the 19th century roses were often dipped in paraffin to delay their deterioration. This doesn't really dry them and the life span of a paraffin dipped rose is usually less than three weeks.

Other Uses for Roses

Because the rose is the most recognized floral scent in the world and the most recognized flower in the United States, it has been used in a multitude of commercial products and preparations. These include the use of fresh petals or rose oils in the production of rose soaps, candles, potpourri, perfumes and hair care products. Pressed flowers and petals are popular for notecards, picture frames, book covers and more. Today there is great interest in the scent of roses in aromatherapy.

Rose beads

This is an ancient art and a great project for kids. Beads have played an important part in our sense of adornment, but in earlier days, when there were no written languages, or there were few people who could read, beads were a memory trigger, a way of counting, a way of keeping track of time, wealth, and prayers. Almost all of the world's religions have used beads at one time or another, from the rosary of the Catholic faithful to the prayer beads of Muslims and Hindus.

BEYOND THE ROSE GARDEN

There are some claims that the rosary was so named because it represented the vision of St. Dominic, who saw the prayer as a wreath or garland of roses. Others claim that it refers to the original rosaries which were carved from wood into the shape of rose blossoms. During the Middle Ages beads for the rosaries of the poor peasants were made from rose petal paste, giving them both a comforting fragrance and affordability.

For rose beads you can send the kids out to gather a plastic grocery bag full of assorted rose petals. Use a food processor or blender to turn them into a thick paste. You may want to spread this paste on a plate to dry over night then blend it a second time. It needs to dry to the consistency of Play-Doh.® Then the little people in your life can begin to roll out beads of various sizes and shapes. You can string them on a coarse thread or pin each bead to a piece of cardboard with a straight pin. Either way they have to dry for a week or two until they are solid. The beads can then be polished and faceted or painted. When strung on a necklace these hard beads will release their fragrance for years and can last for generations.

Rose water

Rose water was a basic condiment, cosmetic, medicine and household item in the earlier days of this country as well as a tradition throughout Europe, India and much of Asia Minor. There are many ways to make your own rose water. Some are as simple as adding fresh rose petals to cold water and bringing to a boil. Other experts insist that it isn't rose water unless it is distilled. The following was taken from a book published in London in 1762 titled *The Toilet of Flora*.

> The TOILET of FLORA;
> or A COLLECTION of the Methods Most Simple and Approved
> FOR THE USE OF THE LADIES
> **improved from the French work of M. Buchoz, M.D.**
>
> 34 To make rofe-water
> To make an excellent rofe-water, let the flowers be gathered two or three hours after fun rising in very fine weather, beat in the mortar into a pafte, leave then in the mortar foaking in their juice, for five or fix hours, then put the mafs into a coarfe canvas bag, and prefs out the

PART THREE

> juice; to every quart of Juice add a pound of fresfh Damafk Rofes, and let them ftand in the infufion for twenty four hours; then put the whole into a glafs alembic, lute on a head and receiver, and place it in a fand heat ; diftill at firft with a gentle fire, which is to be encreafed gradually till the drops follow each other as quick as poffible ; draw off the water as long as it continues to run clear, then put out the fire, and let the alembic ftand till cold. The diftilled water at firft will have very little fragrancy, but after being expofed to the heat of the fun about eight days, in a bottle lightly ftopped with a bit of paper, it foon acquires an admirable fcent.

They must have had more time on their hands back then. Many recipes call for the addition of rubbing alcohol. Don't do this if you are going to use the rose water in cooking or the preparation of drinks.

Roses on the Dinner Table

> *An idealist is one who, on noticing that roses smell better than cabbage, conclude that it will also make better soup.*
>
> H. L. Mencken

We are accustomed to seeing roses used as a centerpiece on the table in a fine restaurant, or to celebrate special occasions on our own dining room table. Yet, this is only one way that roses can appear on the table. To make your meal a truly unique and memorable event roses can be a part of the meal, a key ingredient in both the food and drink, even the dessert. Yes! You can take time to eat the roses, as well as smell them.

Entire cookbooks have been written on roses, recipes for everything from rose scented tea to scrambled eggs with rose petals. Recipes for rose flavored ice cream can also be found. Cooking with roses is nothing new. In fact, it is a tradition as old as our human fascination with the rose, dating back beyond the days of the Roman Empire, or the Egyptians before the pyramids. Some sources claim that the oldest rose recipe is from ancient Rome and was for a rose candy. During the heyday of the Persian Empire rose water was a basic flavoring for everything from wine to bread. Medieval

Europe didn't have access to many of the herbs and spices we have today, but they grew roses in profusion and made tea from the leaves, flowers and hips. They flavored fish, beef and chicken with roses. Rose petals flavored puddings, butters, pastries, soups, stews, honeys, vinegars and oils. Rose flavored condiments were as much a part of the table setting as salt and were more commonly available than pepper.

Many of the historic rose recipes were handed down from generation to generation or were a traditional food item of an entire village or province. The use of roses as a food source isn't just European. Asians, Africans and even American Indians enjoyed the delightful and delicate and varied flavors to be found in roses. As people migrated from continent to continent and cultures were shared, new ways of preparing food were discovered, recipes were modified and tastes changed. This is a process that continues today, because food is one of the basic human adventures and many of us are adventurous enough to treat our tastebuds to something new.

There was also a medicinal value ascribed to rose petals and hips. They are full of vitamins and minerals. Not only do roses taste good, they can be a key ingredient in a healthy diet.

Before you munch the rose petals

Never use rose petals, leaves or hips that have been sprayed with pesticides unless you are absolutely certain they were safe for human consumption. This isn't something you want to guess about.

I suggest that you use only the roses from bushes you have been growing in your own landscape, that you know haven't been treated with sprays, dusts, weed-&-feed products or systemic pesticides. If you grew it, you know what's in it.

Harvesting roses for the dinner table

- Most rose petals are most flavorful if you harvest them early in the morning.
- Mature, fully open roses tend to be more flavorful than rosebuds. Rose buds can sometimes be bitter.
- Pink and red roses hold their color best when used in the kitchen. Yellow, orange and white flowers tend to turn brown or

PART THREE

rust colored.
- Separate the petals and rinse before using.
- Taste a raw petal or two before using them in a recipe. In some varieties the tip of the petal, where it attaches to the rest of the flower, can be bitter. Simply pinch this off before using if this is a problem.

These are among the best Florida roses for dining.
They are fragrant, flavorful and hold color well.

Belinda's Dream	Chrysler Imperial
Louis Phillippe	Mrs. B. R. Cant
Duchesse de Brabant	Souvenir de la Malmaison
Don Juan	Catherine Nelson

> My Uncle Earl used to sprinkle rose petals on pancakes at the Apopka Rotary Club pancake dinner, and he got rave reviews for this tasty treat.

Basic rose petal sweet sauce

Rose sauces were popular throughout Europe and the Mediterranean basin. The original sweeteners were probably honey, maple syrup or beet sugar, but you can use our commonly available granulated sugar. This is a simple sauce that can be used as a topping, key ingredient in desserts, drinks, jellies, preserves, baking and so much more. You can use your favorite sauce recipe if you wish. This is a basic one that works well.

In a large saucepan blend a quart of cold water and 6 to 10 cups of fresh, washed rose petals. Bring to almost a boil, then let sit until the liquid is cool and strain through a cloth. The resulting rose water can be used as the liquid in your favorite sweet sauce recipe. This liquid will remain flavorful for three or four days if kept refrigerated. This is the easy way to do it. Many of the experts recommend something along the lines of the following. The flavor is slightly different when this recipe is used.

Begin with 1½ cup of sugar and ½ cup of corn syrup in a saucepan with 2 cups of water. Simmer to dissolve and blend the sugar. After this syrup is ready, add 2 to 4 cups of fresh, washed rose petals for each cup of liquid and bring to a boil. You may want to add a teaspoon or two of lemon juice to the mix as well. Remove from heat when the desired color has been obtained, and the sauce begins to thicken slightly. Red rose petals will make the preserves dark pink or red, pink roses will produce a lighter shade of pink.

Strain the petals from the syrup for a clear sauce, although some recipes call for keeping the rose petals in the mix. This can be done, but often the rose petals will discolor slightly and continue to darken the color of the sauce. If you are using rose petals for flavoring it isn't necessary to add other spices such as cinnamon, allspice or cloves.

This sauce can be used as a topping on everything from ice cream and pudding to cakes and pies. It can also be used as a dip for fruit and vegetables, mixed with apple sauce, poured over blackberries or blueberries. This rose petal sweet sauce can also be used as a glaze for ham and a marinade for chicken. It makes a delightfully different glaze for sweet potatoes, baked potatoes, carrots, onions and other vegetables.

It can also be used in a thinner mix when canning peaches, pears, spiced apples, jams, preserves, more. Use your imagination.

Roses as a spice in jellies, jams, preserves and conserves

Rather than give you detailed instruction on how to make jams, jellies and other sweet preserves, we would like to suggest that you simply modify your own favorite recipe by using the above rose sweet sauce. Peaches, pears and apples work the best, but rose & berry preserves can also be a taste treat. A simple rose preserve without the fruit is also great.

Rose honey was a favorite on the Victorian dinner table. This recipe was taken from the Agriculturalist's Almanac for 1886. "Excellent rose-honey is made by bringing 1 part fresh rosewater and 1 part raw honey to a good simmer 'till sufficiently reduced. Then filter and use for both salubrious effect and fine flavor."

Rose vinegar was used as a salad dressing and as flavoring in cooking throughout the colonial period of our country. The finest rose vinegars were made from distilled white vinegar, but almost any type of vinegar was flavored with rose petals. Often times other herbs such as tarragon, mint, savory, and thyme were blended with the rose petals.

PART THREE

This is the way most of them started. A loosely packed cup of fresh red or pink rose petals is placed in a container containing approximately ½ gallon of good vinegar. It then is sealed tightly and placed in a cool dark place for 2 to 4 weeks. After this "curing time" the rose-vinegar is strained to remove the rose petals and it is poured into decorative vinegar bottles. Often a tight pink rose bud was added to each bottle.

Rose butter was also a popular item on the Victorian table. It was considered a pure delight on hot, fresh baked bread. The creation of a fine rose butter required effort. There were several methods popular. One recipe simply called for the blending of a cup and a half of red rose petals to a pound of fresh salted cream butter. This yielded a pink butter that would keep for about three days before the petals turned brown.

Another recipe called for the "blending of ½ cup of distilled rose-water and one pound of soft fresh butter, whipping until it is of a soft consistency, easily spread." It was to be served immediately because the rose water would separate from the butter if it was left standing.

The most involved recipe called for the crushing of "four cups of fresh gathered petals of fine and fragrant rose in a mortar until paste. Blend this thoroughly into two pounds of butter fresh churned. Turn into rose butter molds and chill on ice or in spring house until firmly chilled. Serve with garnish of rose or mint leaves."

Rose flavored sugars were a popular table item in the not too distant past. Cinnamon sugar, mint sugar and rose sugar were the most popular. This is an easy project for the kids. Take ½ cup of diced rose petals per cup of white sugar. Mix together and store in a sealed container for two or three weeks. Then sift to remove the dried rose petals and you have rose flavored sugar.

Rose cream cheese is easy to make. Simply blend some rose petals into sour cream or cream cheese and let stand over night for a delightful flavor that can add so much to everything from bagels to baked potatoes. You can even use some rose water if you would rather. One warning is in order. The rose petals will turn brown and, while still healthy, may not look as appetizing as you might like.

Roseye was a popular meat sauce throughout Europe during the middle ages. This sauce was flavored with a blend of roses and almonds and was used to enhance a wide variety of fish, fowl and wild game dishes. In England it was served with eel.

In those good old days it was made with lard, flour and water. Today you can use corn starch as the thickening agent. Begin by making a sauce base with a couple of tablespoons of corn starch and about a cup of water, add a good handful of ground, toasted almonds and simmer, stirring constantly until it begins to thicken. Rather than a mortar and pestle you can use the blender or food processor to make a paste from about a cup of red or pink rose petals and small handful of crushed toasted almonds. Gradually add the rose petal paste to the thickening agent until it is blended well. It doesn't need to come to a boil. If it becomes too thick you can add milk, sour cream or water to thin the sauce to the desired consistency. This sauce also works well on baked potatoes and other vegetables.

Nothin' says loving like roses from the oven. Roses can make a great flavoring for breads, biscuits, cookies, cakes, pies and almost anything else you might choose to bake. Most of these recipes call for the addition of a teaspoon or two of rose water as the flavoring. If you are truly daring you can even add a handful of petals or two. While rose petal bread is great, one of the best taste treats is the old German rose-water sugar cookie that continues to be a popular tradition in some families.

You can use your own favorite basic sugar cookie recipe and simply add ½ teaspoon of rose water per cup of flour. If you use rose water made from red rose petals, a pink blush will be evident in the finished product. If you want to go to extremes you can garnish each cookie with a candied rose petal.

Rose flavored potatoes are a delight. The potato is, by itself, a bland and rather uninteresting food. But it has the advantage of accepting and blending a wide range of other flavors. Dill, parsley, tarragon and chives are only a few of the great herbs we commonly find used with potatoes. Rose petaled potatoes are also a great treat. Mashed potatoes can become truly unique when a cup of fresh red rose petals are added as you begin the mashing process. Baked potatoes can be splashed with rose water or covered with rose flavored sour cream.

PART THREE

Rose petal soup was popular in the France of Louis the XIV. It was made by first preparing a creamed vegetable soup using carrots, parsnips, celery, parsley and onions. As the soup is about to be served, for each quart of soup, 1/4 cup of rose water was added. Then a handful of fresh rose petals in a variety of colors was scattered over the soup bowl and plate. Variations called for the addition of several cups of fresh petals to the soup while simmering.

Pear-Rose soup is a natural because pears and roses go together so well. The French produced entire books of rose-pear recipes. A pear-rose soup was a court favorite and continued to be enjoyed through the Napoleonic years. "Pears are diced, then boiled in just sufficient rose water to cover them until soft. These pears and rose water are mashed along with a handful of ground, toasted almonds. A variety of spices such as cardamom, ginger, allspice, cloves or cinnamon can be added. Bring the whole to a simmer, stirring constantly until it commence thickening. Remove from heat and strain for clarity, Chill and serve with garnish of colorful rose petals and sprigs of mint."

The rose blossom was considered just another vegetable. A simple method of preparing vegetables often used by the French peasant class was boiling. It was common practice to add handfuls of rose petals to the pot while they boiled green beans, carrots, asparagus, greens, peas or onions. In the Orient rose petals are sometimes used to flavor rice.

There are entire books filled with rose recipes from all over the world and dating back thousands of years.

Rose petal tea, hot or cold. Iced teas are a delight with the addition of a hint of rose. Prepare tea as you would normally do and add a handful of fresh rose petals per pint of water. The petals release some of the flavor during the brewing process even in you use the sun tea method.

When brewing a cup of regular tea, or using a tea bag, a few rose petals add a delicious of flavor. Dried petals can also be used but a slightly different flavor is obtained.

It is possible to brew a quality tea with just rose petals, ignoring the tea bags altogether. Use ½ cup of fresh or dried rose petals for every three cups of water. Bring the water to the boiling point, remove from the heat and pour over the leaves. Let steep for about 10 minutes and enjoy.

Rose Hips are the berries or seed capsules of the rose. Hips are what happens when you don't deadhead the rose bushes. They are also one of the world's best sources of vitamin C. During WWII the British collected tons of rose hips and made them into syrups to supply their troops as a preventative for scurvy and general health. They can add a tangy, sweet flavor to a wide variety of foods and drinks.

The best source for rose hips is Rosa rugosa. Unfortunately it doesn't grow well in Florida, but almost all roses will produce some hips. In Florida Carefree Beauty is one of the most prolific producers of rose hips.

Rose hips can be used to make tea, can be added to soups, fruit dishes, jellies and preserves, sauces, cheese spreads, added to breads and other baked goods, or utilized almost any way that the petals were used in the previous pages. In both Russia and Sweden a traditional wine was made from rose hips.

Harvesting and preparing rose hips:
- It's best to wait until they are fully ripe & slightly soft, to harvest.
- Wash the hips well to remove dust and dirt.
- Remove the blossom end & stem ends with scissors or a knife.
- Cut lengthwise and remove the seeds and fine hairs. Note: these hairs can cause irritation to the mouth, throat and stomach if swallowed. Strain the tea before drinking, then enjoy.

Rose leaves were also used in cooking and the preparation of vinegars. Fine Turkish chefs prepared a rose leaf jelly that was considered a delicacy. In the Orient they use young rose leaves in soups, make teas with the leaves at all stages of maturity. There were many medicinal uses for rose leaves in cultures from ancient Egypt to China and the villages of American Indians.

PART THREE

Healing with Roses

From the scent of roses used by the Sumarians as an aphrodisiac to the Egyptians who used rose petals in the tombs of their dead, roses have been valued for more than their beauty. In fact, all over the world they have been valued as a medicinal herb. We find rose hips at the corner drug store today, as well as herbal teas containing rose hips, petals and leaves.

Rose honey was a popular treatment for the general weakness, those suffering from melancholy, colic or consumption, and those fevered and with sore throat. Rose hip teas were also prescribed by the Dr. Moms of the Middle Ages.

Red roses were recommended to strengthen the heart. Teas, powders and syrups of rose hips were used to control internal bleeding, coughs and scurvy. A wash made from white roses was used for inflammations of the eyes and skin.

Sweet rose water was used with smelling salts to refresh the faint, and handkerchiefs were soaked with the attar of roses to sniff as a cure for drowsiness. The scent of fresh roses was said to awaken the senses and make one mentally alert.

In North America the native population used rose hips in soups and teas to treat colds and sore throats.

There are entire books written exploring the medicinal value of roses, and how they have been used in the healing arts throughout history.

Another quiz

Who Said That About Roses?

What a perfect subject for literary metaphor is the rose. Absolute in its beauty, exquisite in its ability to seduce humanity, the perfume of the gods and the symbol of paradise; yet it is gangly in form, its charm defended by thorns. So much a reflection of life itself is this flower that writers, wordsmiths and poets all have harvested thoughts from the rose garden. How well can you match these great

BEYOND THE ROSE GARDEN

lines with the immortal, or immoral poets who penned them?

1. *A rose is a rose is a rose.*   a) Sir Thomas Moore

2. *'Tis the last rose of summer*   b) George Eliot
   Left blooming alone;
   All her lovely companions   c) Gertrude Stein
   Are faded and gone;
   No flower of her kind   d) William Shakespeare
   No rosebud is nigh;
   To reflect back her blushes,   e) E. B. Yeats
   Or give sigh for sigh.
       f) Robert Herrick

3. *Red rose, proud rose, sad rose*
      of all my days!
   Come near me, while I sing
      the ancient ways.

4. *It will never rain roses: when we want*
   To have more roses we must plant more trees

5. *Gather ye rose-buds while ye may*
    Old time is still a-flying:
   And this same flower that smiles today,
   Tomorrow will be dying.

6. *Roses have thorns, and silver fountains mud;*
   Clouds and eclipses stain the moon and sun,
   And loathsome canker lives in sweetest bud
   All men make faults

PART THREE

Answers to Who Said That About Roses?

1. Gertrude Stein, *Geography and Plays*

2. Sir Thomas Moore, *Last Rose of Summer*

3. William Butler Yeats, *The Rose of Battle*

4. George Eliot, *The Spanish Gypsy*

5. Robert Herrick

6. William Shakespeare, *35th Sonnet*

Part 4
Roses in Myth, Legend and History

Rose Myths and Legends

Origin of the rose

For the origins of the rose, a flower of mythological proportions, we go back to the beginnings of Roman history. In those days athere were no roses. There was, however, a beautiful young lady named Rhodanthe. So beautiful was this Roman maiden that all the young men in the city were smitten, as were a goodly number of the older and married men as well. They pursued her, courted her, wined and dined her, took her to the theater, on picnics, to sporting events and to the beach (They never made it to Disney World, however).

She became exhausted from all this attention and sought help from her friends in high places. Diana was the goddess of wisdom. She also held the title of goddess of the hunt. She lived in a huge temple with stone walls and great Italian oak doors. Diana suggested that Rhodanthe hide out for a while in the temple. Attendance at the temple more than doubled as the menfolk of the city discovered that Rhodanthe had taken a part time job as a vestal virgin. Diana was a bit jealous and closed the doors to the temple. That's when the trouble really started.

The suitors gathered into a mob and stormed the temple gates, crashing through the heavy oak doors and making a mess of the floors inside. They drank the wine, walked all over the furniture and really trashed the place. This changed Diana's jealousy about Rhodanthe's popularity into real anger. Making Diana mad was sorta like messin' with Mama Nature. She entered the courtyard, and being a goddess, waved her arms and turned her former friend into a rose bush and all of the suitors into thorns. This was the way the rose was born. It's also one myth of how the rose got its thorns.

Why Rose has Thorns

In early days of the Roman civilization roses were of a pink color, thornless, single in form and fragrant beyond belief. Truly a flower to be admired, but it wasn't until a mishap occurred that the flower became associated with romance and became the very symbol of love.

Back in those days Venus was the goddess of love, and she had a son, Cupid. He was out in the yard, playing with a toy bow and arrow that his parents had given him for his birthday. He had just cocked the arrow and was taking aim on a sunbeam when a bee stung him. The arrow missed its target and landed in a distant rose garden. From that day on roses had thorns, as a symbolic sting from Cupid's arrow. Later, while Venus was taking a relaxing stroll through the same rose garden, she pricked her foot on one of the thorns and a drop of her pure red blood was shed. It was this drop of blood from the toe of Venus that turned the roses red and also turned them into the symbol of love. The rose possessed the beauty and allure of Venus and the sting or pain of youthful love from her son, Cupid's, arrow. This is why roses have had thorns ever after.

The Story of the White Rose

Venus was linked to another rose legend. This time it's the origin of the white rose. It seems that Venus, the Roman goddess of love and beauty, was deeply in love with the perfect man, Adonis. When this love of her life was gone she mourned and grieved inconsolably. Weeping continuously, she shed rivers of tears for her beloved wherever she went. Everywhere that a tear fell a bush of white roses grew. This is generally not the way we propagate roses today.

Queen of the Flowers

The Greek poet, Sappho, called the rose "the Queen of Flowers" in 600 BC. This is a brief version of the Greek origin of the rose.

ROSES IN MYTH, LEGEND & HISTORY

Before the Romans and the story of Rhodanthe, the Greeks had a love affair with roses that had been going on for centuries. Their story of the origin of the rose began with Choris, the Greek goddess of flowers. She was taking a stroll through the woods one day and found a dead nymph. She took this little lifeless body back to Mount Olympus, the housing development where all the gods and goddesses lived. There she called all of her friends over to see what they could do with this poor foundling.

Aphrodite, the goddess of love and the most beautiful of all the goddesses, took out her makeup kit and went to work on the rather plain looking nymph. Beauty creams, eye shadow, a little lipstick and blush were applied. Aphrodite gave the nymph the beauty of a flower.

Dionysus, the god of wine, shared a bottle of his finest vintage with the assembled gods and goddesses. The few drops that were left he dripped onto the body of the nymph. This was the best wine available from the Mt. Olympus Winery, delicate of flavor, rich in color and intoxicatingly fragrant, great bouquet. This became the nectar, the fragrance, the allure of a flower that was to be.

The three graces brought their gifts of charm, brightness and joy. These were the qualities that support a good life. Without them all is dreary, dull and depressing.

Zephyr, also called West Wind, with one great breath blew away the dark and dismal clouds to open the blue sky. Zephyr decreed that a light breeze should always accompany this nymph that was rapidly being transformed into a delightfully beautiful creature. With this breeze the fragrance of Dionysus' wine-nectar would announce its approach.

Apollo was the god of the sun. He saw all the commotion going on at Aphrodite's house and dropped in to see what was happening. When he saw the now beautiful body lying on the bed he called the sun to shine brightly and illuminate this creature. With this solar radiance the nymph stirred and flexed its arms. As it moved the arms became branches. The graces gifts of charm, brightness and joy became shiny green leaves while the face became the most beautiful of flowers. The rose was born. Zeus was out walking his dog and walked past Aphrodite's place, saw everyone gathered and thought there was a party going on that he hadn't been invited to.

PART 4

A bit miffed, he entered and saw the beautiful flower before him. He declared it the "Queen of Flowers" and decreed that it live forever and grow all over the world.

It seems that the Greek gods and goddesses couldn't bring the dead back to life, but they could recycle them into something else. One thought to leave you with. It appears from this story that the rose was the product of a committee. Perhaps we shouldn't be too critical of committees; some do pretty good work.

The Christmas Rose

This story begins on a cold clear night over two thousand years ago. On this night a poor carpenter and his wife were stranded in a small town called Bethlehem. This was in the days before Motel 6, Holiday Inn or even a homeless shelter. The only place available, the only place they could afford was a space in a stable. On that night this carpenter's wife gave birth to a baby boy and he was placed in a hay manger.

This doesn't seem like something that would appear on CNN, but off in the hills outside the city, angels appeared out of nowhere and began talking to the shepherds that were tending their flocks. The angels told these shepherds that this birth was a special occasion and that they had something to celebrate. Being kind, considerate country folk, they selected gifts from their meager possessions and went to visit this new family with presents of food, clothing, warm woolen blankets. Simple gifts from people who lived a simple life.

Back in those days many of the shepherds were actually shepherdesses and they also brought gifts. All except one who was so poor that she had no blanket to give, not even a morsel of food to share. She sat and wept. So sorrowful was she that she had no gift to give that she sobbed great tears so that the ground was wet from them. There was a bright flash of light. When she looked up, an angel was standing in front of her. The angel knelt and put an arm around her and asked the reason for her sadness. After the young shepherdess gave an explanation between choking sobs, the angel held her hand and they prayed together.

As they stepped back from the soil wet with her tears, a wondrous thing began to happen. From the barren earth a bush began to grow. As the girl watched, in the radiance from the angel, stems and leaves formed, then deep red flower buds appeared at the tip of each branch. As the angel faded, the shepherdess took her knife and cut a bouquet of a dozen roses, left her flock and walked down the hill toward the stable.

She didn't bring the gifts of food, clothing and household goods like her friends, but she brought something just as important, for she gave the gift of beauty.

One version of this story, circulated, I suspect by the Rose Growers Council, claims that the infant reached out to touch the rose while ignoring the gold, frankincense and myrrh.

A Brief History of the King of Flowers

Ancient Egypt

Roses were popular in Egypt at least 5000 years ago and probably thousands of years earlier. It was used both as a food source and for its beauty and fragrance. Bouquets were offered Isis the Egyptian goddess of fertility. Other civilizations throughout the Fertile Crescent also enjoyed roses, filling gardens and royal palaces with them. For some it was a flower chosen by the gods, for others it was considered the domain of kings alone. Cleopatra was rumored to have entertained Marc Anthony on a bed of rose petals.

Early China

The Chinese were experts at rose cultivation almost as long ago as the Egyptians. Some varieties were only for the court, others belonged to the people. In 500 BC the Imperial library contained hundreds of books on roses. The Chinese carefully guarded their rose varieties and growing techniques from the rest of the world for centuries. It was with the introduction of these Chinese roses into Europe, where they were crossed with those traditional species, that the modern rose was born.

India

The rose has been a tradition in the Indian subcontinent for untold centuries. Being at the crossroads of the East and the West, the Indian cultures knew well the roses of much of the world. It was the Indians who first developed the technique for producing attar of roses. In the Hindu traditions, Laxmi, the goddess of wealth was born from a rose flower. Extensive and well cared for rose gardens were a part of the good life of India for thousands of years.

Both India and Pakistan were traditional sources of rose perfumes and rose oil. There is a wealth of myths and legends about the origin of attar of roses. One gives credit to an Indian princess, Nar Mahal, who filled a pond with rose petals and took her husband on a boat ride into this romantic setting. The hot Indian sun, beating down on this flotilla of rose petals released the fragrance into the air around their boat, but they soon noticed something more. There was an oil slick forming on the surface of the water. When Nur Mahal dipped her finger into this oil she found it was the pure essence of rose. She was so thrilled with her discovery that she forgot all about the romantic interlude with her husband and called for her servants, instructing them to use cotton sponges to recover the oil and bottle it. A new industry came into being.

Classical Greece

The rugged rose was no stranger to the coasts and hillsides of Greece. As cited above, a multitude of Greek myths and legends centered on the rose. It was also a part of the culture, finding a home on the temple grounds of gods and goddesses and in the gardens of the kings and scholars. Roses were also used much as we do today, as tokens of affection, in bouquets, corsages, table decor, funeral wreaths and the crowns of victorious athletes. Theofratus described dozens of varieties of rose in his book *Enquiry into Plants*. Alexander the Great carried roses into battle, and the bedroom. For the Greek physician the rose was a part of the pharmacy, for the chef it was kept on the spice shelf.

Rome

Nero is often portrayed as a cruel, selfish and gluttonous fool. The fact is he really knew how to throw a party, and he partied often. The rose was one of the favorites of the Roman high society and the excesses of these party animals was often linked to the simple rose. Cushions and pillows were stuffed with both fresh and dried rose petals, floors were covered sometimes over a foot deep with rose petals. The fountains were filled with rose scented water. This fragrance of rose water was also pink in color and changed shades as it flowed illuminated by candles.

They even bathed in pools of rose scented water that had bushels of rose petals floating on the surface. They ate rose cakes, drank rose flavored wine and enjoyed rose custards and puddings for dessert. In the winter they even had rose flavored ice and the Roman version of Sno-cones.

The rose was used as an element of decor, a source of fragrance, and a symbol of opulence. The degree to which roses were in presence was an indication of the social or political standing of the guests.

When political dealing was going on, participants sat under a rose suspended from the ceiling, to signify that what was said was "off the record." Today we have the legal term *sub rosa* that is a carryover of this classic Roman custom.

Persia

Today we call it Iran, is often credited with bringing the rose back into popularity after the decline and fall of the Roman Empire. They cultivated many varieties of roses, developed the perfume trade and increased the demand for both the plants and the products made from roses. The truth is however that the rose was a staple item during the middle Ages, sometimes called the Dark Ages of European history. The rose was popular and widely planted throughout Europe during this time and was grown for the beauty as well as the medicinal value of the hips. It was in this time period that the rosary, rose windows in cathedrals and the rose as a frequent object of art became popular.

Persians, reveling in their own version of the "Life styles of the Rich and Famous," slept on beds of rose petals, changed daily, covered the streets with rose petals in a Persian version of a tickertape parade, and coated their bodies with rose oil to prevent the wrinkles of aging.

England

With roses being such a popular flower all over the world, it

PART 4

was to be expected that it would become the symbol of warring factions somewhere. From 1455 (actually the dispute began in 1399) to 1487 England was engaged in a series of civil wars called The War of the Roses. The House of York, carrying the white rose, was disputing the House of Lancaster, the guys with the red roses. The bloody squabbling continued with the House of York in the throne most of the time, until Henry Tudor, one of the red rose guys, finally defeated Richard III at Bosworth Field in 1485 to found a new dynasty. Minor battles continued for a couple years after, but finally everybody got tired of fighting and settled down to grow roses instead — a tradition David Austin continues to this day.

The rose reached fad proportions some time later. Roses and rose water became legal tender. Rent was often paid in rose water or rose hips, as was one's loyalty.

France
The French in the 1600's established great formal rose gardens, initiated the concept of rose hybridization and scoured the earth for new wild varieties. They introduced the Chinese repeat bloomers to the European continent. Josephine, Napoleon's wife, had an extensive rose garden and grew over 250 varieties. It was at her residence, Chateau de Malmaison, that the famous French artist, Pierre

A Brief History of Roses in America

Redoute did his collection of rose paintings.
In the Beginning
The global story of the rose begins in what is now Florissant, Colorado about 40 million years ago. The earliest evidence of this great family is found in the shale deposits of several sites in the Western United States, including Montana and Oregon. This earliest known ancestor makes the rose truly an American original, a native plant, a fitting symbol of this nation and its people. While all the continents except Antarctica claim native roses, we can boast the oldest.

ROSES IN MYTH, LEGEND & HISTORY

Dateline Atlantic Ocean, Oct 11, 1492
Chris Columbus was lost, stuck in the dead calm of the Sargasso Sea and facing a mutiny from his sailors. His horoscope said today was a good day to give up and stay in bed. Then a rose entered the picture. That afternoon a sailor pulled a branch from a wild briar rose out of the water. There were no leaves left, but it bore the red fruit well known to these seafarers. A rose branch meant that land must be near, and the next day they spotted it. While this may well be an historic myth, and the first sign of land was probably birds, it is plausible and possible that a briar could have been floating in the currents.

In the Colonies
It is interesting to note that there were accounts from both the Virginia colony and the Massachusetts Bay Colony of native roses growing in abundance. In Virginia Capt John Smith was surprised to find that the Virginia Indians had planted roses around their villages as a thing of beauty, and also for the edible fruit, flowers and leaves. The rose was perhaps the first ornamental cultivated by the colonists. It should be kept in mind that the rose to these people was both a medicinal herb and an ornamental.

When William Penn settled Pennsylvania he also planted a personal rose garden with varieties he brought over from England in 1699. In the early 1700s land was rented out by the Penn family with the payment being a red rose payable annually.

Before there were rose gardens in Pennsylvania the French settlements in Canada and the Great Lakes region were already growing some of the favorites of the French court. Samuel Champlain is credited with bringing the first domesticated roses to North America. In the early 1600s he also took some of the North American natives back to France.

Presidential Rose Growers
Both Washington and Jefferson grew roses on their plantations. George Washington is often referred to as America's first rose breeder. It was John and Abigail Adams who started the White House rose garden in 1800. Actually it was a combined vegetable

PART 4

and ornamental garden with roses. However, it remained for Mrs. Woodrow Wilson to actually design the now famous rose garden that is located outside the president's office.

The Cherokee Rose

The Cherokee Rose is the state flower of Georgia. This is a rugged plant with large single white flowers. The sprawling canes will ramble over 20 feet and in the wild they will form thickets, or briar patches that would make Brer Rabbit deliriously happy. They are once bloomers, filling the early summer air with their spicy fragrance as the mass of white makes the area appear covered with lacy clouds.

There is a legend about this rose and the infamous Trail of Tears. When gold was discovered in the mountains of North Carolina and Georgia, the Cherokee Indians were forced to move to Oklahoma. This forced march became known as the Trail of Tears and thousands of the Cherokee people died on the journey. A legendary link between the rose that bears the Cherokee Nation's name and the people was formed during this dark journey. This story has been told in many ways, by many storytellers, in many versions, in many books. The following is an abbreviated version that, hopefully you will enjoy.

The great march had started in early summer. The Indians had to walk most of the time and this was a hardship for the elderly and the young. The military force assigned the task of moving an entire nation into exile wasn't overly sympathetic to these people who were forced to abandon their homeland. There was occasional conflict and numerous deaths, but it was the hardship of the march itself that caused many of the deaths of the elderly and the children. The loss of dignity, the sense of powerlessness, the sorrow of leaving all that was familiar tore at the heart of the people.

The elders knew that to fight was useless and would only end in the destruction of their people. The wailing of the women, their tears literally soaking the ground they walked over, and the suffering of the children only intensified the desperation. Gathered around the campfire one night these elders, the leaders of their people, talked of the need to give their women strength. If the women of any nation falter, the entire population stumbles and loses its way. They called on the Great Spirit to comfort these people and give their women a sign, so that they might keep the Cherokee people whole to rebuild their nation.

In a vision the Great Mystery spoke, "I see the sorrow of the wives, daughters, sisters and mothers. When they wake in the morning they will find a new plant growing where they tears have fallen the night before. This plant will grow as they feed it with their faith and hope. It will produce long branches that take root and grow, just as the Cherokee people will take root and grow wherever you are."

The Great Mystery continued to speak through the smoke of the fire to these elders wise enough to seek wisdom, "Look closely at the leaves of this new plant and you will see that I have given it seven parts to remind you of the seven nations of the Cherokee. You will also see that this new plant is not only growing along the trail you are taking, it is also growing back along the trail you have traveled. It is growing back into the land of the Cherokee people, to ever remind all that this was of the People. As this plant who is grown from the spirits of all who have been lost on this Trail of Tears reclaims the land of the People it shall be armed with thorns to defend it against all who would remove the People from their land again."

The elders nodded and thanked the Great Mystery for this gift, but one asked, "What you give us is a secret of the Cherokee people, a sign of our place, but will this truly bring joy to our wives, daughters, sisters and mothers?"

"For all the women who have been weeping their loss, I have added the pure white flowers with five petals to remind them of their home in the universe. There is one petal each for the directions of the wind, North, East, South and West. The fifth petal is to represent the Heavens and the hope of the sunshine." The Great Spirit paused in this for a moment, then continued, "I will add gold dust to the center of this flower to remind all of the greed of those who will destroy their mother earth to gain false wealth."

The elders nodded again, muttering that this was good and that the Great Mystery was indeed caring for them. They started to pass

PART 4

the pipe and speak words of thanks when the Great One spoke again.

"To bring joy to the faces of your women now washed with tears, I will add a pleasant fragrance, to remind them of the goodness that is in the world."

With that, the voice in the flames became silent as the elders continued to discuss what had been revealed to them.

In the morning they awoke their wives, mothers, daughters and sisters and told them to look back on their trail of tears. When they saw the new plant growing they were pleased. The elders told them of the vision, and as the story was told, buds appeared on the branches and flowers formed and opened. The women of the Cherokee people stopped thinking of their sorrow and began to speak of tomorrow, talk of the strength of the children and the People.

A Possible Dream, a Rose Supreme

There has been a multitude of stories, myths and legends developed surrounding a popular and charming rose. This rose was shipped from the House of Meilland, a premier French rose breeder in the summer of 1939. It was known at that time by its number 3-35-40. The Meillands sent cuttings with the buds for grafting to rose growers in Germany, Italy and the United States for tests and trials. Some claim that it departed France as smuggled goods in diplomatic pouches on the last plane to leave before the fall of France.

While this is a great story of intrigue there are many who question the dramatic timing of these events. There were also claims that the fate of the rose in each of these countries was lost in the horror of war. We do know that the Germans called this beautiful rose *Gloria Dei* (Glory of God) and the Italians knew it as *Giola*, translated as "a smile."

Francis Meilland gave us some insight into the history of this rose when he wrote:

"Until June 1945, we had not the least idea as to what had become of this rose in the United States. It was only then that Conard Pyle Company told us of the successful experiments it had been making in cultivating it, and that, in agreement with certain other rose growers of repute, it had been named . . . ."

This rose whose story was so intertwined with the course of history was officially christened in California on April 29, 1945, the day Berlin fell to allied forces, the day history knows as VE Day. We had a rose that was a survivor, a symbol of hope and rugged determination. We also had a rose with an undeniable star quality.

To make the story even more fascinating the United Nations was being formed with delegates meeting in San Francisco. As the delegates, representing the dream of peace on earth for forty-nine countries sat at their table to make their dreams a reality, the American Rose Society had a gift for each of them. Each of these world leaders was given a vase with a single rose in it and a card that said simply,

"This is the Peace rose which was christened at the Pacific Rose Society Exhibition in Pasadena on the day Berlin fell. We hope the Peace rose will influence men's thoughts for everlasting world peace."

The rose we know as *Peace* has been called the most beautiful rose in the world. Everyone recognizes this large yellow rose with the soft blush of pink on the edges of the petals. So popular has this rose been that there are numerous varieties now bearing the Peace name; Chicago Peace, Pink Peace, Climbing Peace and more. Poems have been written about this rose. It has been the darling of both the everyday home gardener and those doing the flower show and exhibition circuit. This "rose of the century," as some have called it, has a certain mystique about it that goes with its fascinating history.

Peace is famous within the world of rose hybridizers for the remarkable lines of modern roses that trace their parentage back to it.

Perhaps this is more than just a rose. Perhaps it is proof that beauty survives. Perhaps it is the symbol of the possible dream. Perhaps it is a prayer for all humanity.

PART 4

Another Rose Quiz
Absolutely Useless Information

1. Where was the great grandiflora rose, Queen Elizabeth developed?
   (A) England
   (B) Scotland
   (C) United States
   (D) Australia

2. Which of the following Presidents does not have a rose named after him?
   (A) George Washington
   (B) Herbert Hoover
   (C) Abraham Lincoln
   (D) John F. Kennedy

 ROSES IN MYTH, LEGEND & HISTORY

3. More roses are _____ than any other color.
   (A) White
   (B) Yellow
   (C) Red
   (D) Pink

4. All red roses are said to have been developed from the roses of
   (A) France
   (B) China
   (C) North America
   (D) England

5. The very first rose patented in the United States, Rose patent # 1, was
   (A) Peace
   (B) Mr. Lincoln
   (C) American Beauty
   (D) New Dawn

Answers: 1. (C), 2. (A), 3. (D), 4. (B), 5. (D)

Part 5
Defining the Rose

A Dictionary of Rose Terms

What's in a name? That which we call a rose
By any other name would smell as sweet.
                                    Bill Shakespeare

AARS, All-American Rose Selection is a non-profit association that, since 1938, has conducted trials and encouraged the rose hybridizers and growers to improve the strength, beauty, fragrance and over all quality of roses. Its awards honor the best roses in the world.

Anthracnose is a fungus disease that looks much like Blackspot. It can attack leaves, stems and fruit. It isn't as common on roses as it is on agricultural crops, but it can be a problem on some climbers. It's most often found in damp weather, during rainy periods and where improper watering practices are used. The best control is still maintenance and good air circulation around and through the plant. In Florida autumn is the deadly season for anthracnose.

Antique rose is a generic term applied to old garden roses as opposed to modern roses. The dividing line is the middle of the 1800s. Often used interchangeably with heritage, historic, shrub and old-fashioned roses.

Apical simply refers to the top or tip of the growing stem. Roses

PART 5

are said to display apical dominance, this means that the flowers are produced at the top rather than along the sides of the stem.

Aphids Insects, usually less than 1/8 inch long, that come in a variety of colors to compliment or accent your favorite roses and their foliage. Tender new growth attracts them like a magnet, and they are truly mathematical geniuses when it comes to multiplication. Ants operate vast aphid ranches where they harvest the sweet excreta that the aphid produces called honeydew. The aphid is the favorite snack food of ladybugs if you are looking for a "law-of-the-jungle" 100% organic insect control. A firm spraying from the water hose also will eliminate the problem.

ARS, American Rose Society. Every plant has its organized group of loyal followers, enthusiasts and fanatics. These are the people that collect, show and set the standards for the industry. The members also provide a tremendous amount of valuable information and capable assistance to individuals who want to grow roses. The ARS was formed in 1892 and is now the largest plant society in the United States. There are more than 20,000 members ranging from university professors and professional growers to homeowners with a plant or two in the back yard. They regulate the naming and registration of rose names and provide a wealth of information.

Attar of roses is the essential oil that is extracted from rose petals. This is used as a base for perfumes, cosmetics and other fragrance products.

Axil in botany is the point of departure for the leaf from the stem. In roses it is the junction of the leaf stem with the cane. This is also the place where *axially buds* arise. These buds become new stems, leaves and flowers, continuing the ever upward and outward growth of the plant.

Balling is a term applied to fully developed buds that fail to open. This can be the result of extremes in weather (wet or cold), or it can be caused by disease damage, usually *Botrytis*, or thrips. The outer petals will stick together and the entire blossom fades or discolors and wilts. It should be noted that some heritage roses are mistakenly described as being susceptible to balling, but this is merely the natural form of the bud and flower that produces lots of delicate petals in a tight bud.

Bare root roses are x-rated roses that are displayed and sold as naked plants without any soil to cover their roots. These are usually dormant plants without green growth that are marketed from mail order sources or discount stores where they are packaged with a sexy picture that lures the customer with promises of what can be theirs if they take this beauty home with them. Some argue that bare root is the safest way to buy because there is less chance of bringing home insect or disease problems that may inhabit the soil. The fact that you have to wait weeks or months for the gratification of a rose in bloom and the other fact that they may in no way resemble the beautiful pictures are good arguments for buying container grown, blooming roses, in particular, those grown in blue pots.

Basal break is a term rose growers use when referring to the new growth that originates from the graft.

Biodegradable refers to materials that will decompose through natural actions of sunlight, bacteria, some insects, earthworms and that multitude of soil organisms that work night and day in your rose garden trying to make it a better world for all of those roots. Many of the chemicals, sprays, soil additives and other materials that we use in gardening aren't biodegradable and can be a source of pollution. The Styrofoam beads that are used in some potting soils, the ties, plastic mulches and even the blue pots are not biodegradable. All parts of plants, animals, even the carcasses of dead bugs are biodegradable. They become first mulch, then compost, then soil. Other materials simply deteriorate by breaking down in to basic chemicals and elements, to be recycled by nature in a multitude of ways.

Black rose A mythical rose offered by numerous mail-order concerns whose operation is unfettered by conscience or integrity. Actually there are a number of nearly black roses on the market, most of which are dark red or purple. If you must have a truly black rose a can of flat black Rustoleum spray paint works well.

Blackspot (or black spot) is a fungus disease that is so named because it actually causes black spots on the leaves of your favorite rose. These spots are usually between 1/16th and ½ inch in diameter. The leaf turns yellow around the spot, dies and drops to become one with the mulch beneath. Blackspot can, if all the conditions for it to live long and prosper are present, seriously defoliate the plant, but this isn't fatal. If you wish to cultivate Blackspot you will have to provide a hot humid atmosphere and leaves that go to bed wet. Over-feeding also encourages this fungus. See page 9 on preventive maintenance to see how this problem can be avoided.

Blasting, shattering Under normal conditions this is a natural part of the life cycle of the flower. After it has brought warmth, good cheer, peace and harmony to the world, this rose is ready to go to seed. The once glorious petals fade, wither and fall in the never-ending cycle of ashes to ashes, or petals to compost. Sometimes it happens before its time and this can be a problem. It can be caused by weather conditions, improper watering, over feeding, improperly applied pesticides, or injury to the plant.

Blind growth is a term used by rosarians in describing a lateral or side shoot that doesn't produce a bud at the apex. This is usually the result of too much fertilizer, or a fertilizer too rich in nitrogen; but it can also be the nature of a variety, such as Bride's Dream.

Blue rose This is something like the quest for the alchemist's stone, the Holy Grail or the black rose. There is no blue rose yet. But the horticultural alchemists are working on it. When we do find the blue rose available in our famous blue pots it will probably be the result of genetic engineering. There are several lavender roses that are called blue, but true blue is still as elusive as the unicorn.

Bluing is what happens to many red and pink roses as they

DEFINING THE ROSE

begin to fade. A blue or lavender coloration begins to show before the petals begin to dry and drop.

Borers These are the larva of several beetles that can invade the freshly pruned rose cane and lay their eggs. The caterpillars simply dine their way deeper and deeper. While not pruning may reduce the number of borers, this can lead to other problems. A coating of the fresh cut with nail polish, good old school glue or a really cheap after shave will discourage the beetles.

Botrytis is often referred to a Botrytis blight. It appears as a gray mold that grows on buds and new growth during periods of wet weather or extreme humidity. This disease causes buds to wither, drop, fail to develop or discolor and fail to open.

Bourbon rose This isn't a reference to the popular rose variety, Whiskey Mac. They are a type of historic or traditional roses from France noted for their compact growth, ruggedness and fragrance. The Bourbon roses were made famous by Marie Antoinette and her artist-rosarian friend, Redoubt.

Buds are the promise of growth to come. They can be buds for leaves, stems or flowers, all waiting for the opportunity to begin the process of growth and maturity. Bud eyes reside at leaf nodes, even after the leaf has continued to the immortal cycle of birth, death and renewal by becoming compost. These bud eyes are patiently waiting for the time when the plant is ready for, or in need of, new canes, branches and leaves. This is what makes bud grafting possible. See also Flower bud

Bud break is the term used to describe the awakening of a dormant bud.

Budding is the process of grafting a bud from the stock (named variety) onto the root stock.

Budded roses are rose plants that are the result of grafting the bud from a named variety onto a rootstock suited for a given cli-

PART 5

mate or conditions. Roses grown from cuttings or seed are said to be on their own root.

Bud union The point of contact between the rootstock and the scion, also called the graft. Above this point the flowers are of the desired, named variety. Growth beneath this point is from the rootstock and will be either *Fortuniana* (if you planted quality Florida grown roses), *Dr. Huey* or *Multiflora*. If the scion dies back to the graft the rootstock will grow with great vigor in an attempt to save itself. Some people say a rose has "reverted back" when this happens.

Calcinated clay is a clay product most often used as kitty litter. It is highly absorbent and is sometimes used as a soil additive when planting roses and other plants and shrubs because it has the ability to hold nutrients and slow the leaching process in our sandy soils. Compost works well and encourages dense root development and the activity of soil borne organisms that make the soil healthy. This clay is sometimes used as the carrier in fertilizer mixes, but when applied as a top dressing it has little value.

Calcium (Ca) Builds strong bones and teeth. Of course this doesn't matter if you are a rose. But it also helps to promote growth, healthy bud formation and stronger cell walls. It helps the plant to handle weather extremes and resist disease. The pelletized slow release fertilizers like Osmocote have calcium in them.

Cambium layer is the living layer of cells between the bark and the wood of the stem. Whether it's a miniature rose or a redwood tree the cambium layer is only one cell thick.

Candelabra is a term used when referring to either the flowers or the way a stem branches. A vigorous cane growing from the graft, or bud union, will produce a number of smaller canes. Often a cluster of flowers that forms with floribundas, polyathas and many of the old roses are said to be candelabra form.

Cane This is what we call the stems of a rose, many berry crops and briars. This is a woody, often unbranched stem that may continue growth from the top (terminal end) until it arches over, touches the ground and takes root. This is characteristic of many wild roses, briars and brambles.

Cane borers (sometimes called crown borers) are the larva of beetles that invade the stem (or cane) of your favorite roses and set up a nursery where they will lay eggs. The egg hatches into a grub or larvae and proceeds to dine on the tender interior wood and leave you with dieback and a pile of sawdust. They will often attack where there has been a fresh cut from your obsession with pruning roses. To control them you can coat fresh cuts or larger canes with fingernail polish, white glue or pruning paint.

Canker is a term used to refer to lesions or diseased areas on the stems of roses. This can be caused by a number of different agents including insects, fungi and chemicals. When the stem is wounded the plant attempts to heal, usually with scar tissue.

Carefree roses are defined as roses that require little or no pesticide sprays, and are low maintenance. These are often old garden roses, antique or heritage roses. They were long overlooked by landscapers and rose growers, but they have been rediscovered and are assuming their logical place in the rose garden and landscape. Nelsons' grows a number of choice carefree roses that are ideal for Florida and the South. All of Nelsons' Carefree roses are grown on Fortuniana rootstock. We can only warn you to beware of varieties that aren't grafted onto Fortuniana rootstock.

Caterpillars are the larva of butterflies or moths. They are generally ugly eating machines that can devour leaves and sometimes flower buds in minutes. They are the favorite snack food in turn of many birds and other insects. They won't kill a plant, even if they totally defoliate it, but they can cause some damage. It's the price we pay for butterflies.

Chelates are chemical compounds that contain needed minerals or trace elements in a form that can be used by the plant. As an example, a rusty nail isn't of any immediate value to your rose bush, but an Iron chelate is.

Cherokee rose is a rose introduced to the Southeast in the early 1800s where it soon went wild. It was sold by nurseries as a living fence for many years. See the legend of the Cherokee rose on page 72.

Chlorophyl is what really makes the world go around. This is the iron based green coloring in the plants' leaves that makes it possible for them to be nature's solar energy machines. This green pigment absorbs energy from the sunlight which is then used in the production of food from carbon dioxide, water and selected nutrients.

Chlorosis is a condition where there is a lack of green color in the leaves of a plant, turning the leaves pale or yellow. This is due to a lack of chlorophyl and can be caused by a number of factors ranging from a lack of nitrogen to overfeeding to too much or too little water. Even cold weather can interrupt the natural nitrogen cycle in many plants, causing chlorosis.

Climbing roses (or climbers) are rose varieties that have extremely long canes that will grow on a support, trellis, fence, arbor or gardener that stands still too long. They often have recurved thorns (prickles to be proper about it) that help to hold the canes in place. Many climbers are sports of hybrid teas or traditional roses, such as the Climbing Peace. Others are traditional climbers like Don Juan and Blossomtime.

Compacted soil is soil that has had much of the air space compressed out of it leaving a fine solid soil that causes water to run off rather than be absorbed. This hard, packed soil can cause poor growth. The best defense against this is to incorporate lots of organic matter into the soil before planting and mulch well after the plants are in the ground. In a healthy soil the multitude of microscopic organisms that Mamma Nature provides work day and night to keep the soil loose. Earthworms will even do their part when they aren't 'gone fishin.'

Compost is what happens when nature takes its course with organic matter. This is the decomposed leaves, grass clippings, peelings and table scraps that can become a valuable soil conditioner and nutrient source that is absolutely safe for your plants and environmentally wise. Most organic mulches such as pine needles or bark chips will decompose into compost and literally percolate down into the soil with time. Don't be upset when the mulch rots away, its building soil for your plants.

Container grown plants are those that are grown in the pot, rather than grown in the field. They tend to have a better root system and there is far less damage in the planting process. Field grown stock can be potted, wrapped in burlap or washed and sold packaged as bare root plants. With container grown plants you can plant any time of the year without transplanting shock and have an instant rose garden.

Corolla a collective term for the petals of a flower.

CR, Consulting rosarian This is a resource available from the American Rose Society. These are rose experts who have a wealth of rose knowledge and are willing to share it. They tend to be a better source of information than the kid that loads the car for you at the garden center.

Crown is the point on the rose plant where the scion and the rootstock have been joined together. This is usually near the soil surface and is characterized by the development of scar tissue in the form of an irregular globe. The crown shouldn't be below the soil surface.

Crown gall is a scaly growth that occurs near the graft on a rose. It's caused by a bacteria.

Cultivar A named variety of plant. Belinda's Dream is a grand example of a rose cultivar. Cultivars are not types or classes of roses, they are the specific named varieties, frequently patented.

Damask roses are antiques dating back to the Crusades. Most Damask varieties are once a year bloomers with a distinctive fragrance. They aren't a great choice for Florida rose gardens.

David Austin Roses Also known as English roses. This is a series of fine roses introduced by the English Rose grower, David Austin in 1969. It is an attempt to combine the best traits of the rugged, classic, old fashioned roses with the dynamics and beauty of modern varieties. What was produced was a number of varieties that had the form and fragrance of a historic rose and the repeat blooming tendencies of today's best. Some of the best for Florida are Abraham Darby and Heritage.

Deadheading is part of the housekeeping we all need to do in the rose garden. This is simply the removal of the faded, or spent, flowers before they begin to set seed. By doing this we can encourage the plant to continue to produce more flower buds.

Debud, disbudding is a practice where secondary flower buds are removed to encourage the plant to put more energy into the production of a single flower. This is often done to produce top quality roses for shows.

Defoliation is the loss of the foliage. This may be due to insects that devour the leaves, fungi like Blackspot, or powdery mildew, or the effects of poor care such as improper watering, over feeding or careless use of pesticides. Leaf loss is not, in itself, fatal. The plant will produce a new display of leaves that are healthy and more efficient at converting sunlight into energy, which is the work leaves do.

Diatomaceous earth (DE) is a naturally occurring soil additive that is composed of the mortal remains of billions and billions of diatoms (microscopic sea life with shells composed of silica.) In a coarse state it is often applied to the soil surface as a control for slugs and snails. Powdered, it's added to soil mixes to help hold water. It is also used in water filters to trap impurities.

Dieback is characterized by the gradual death of twigs, stems and canes, from the tip toward the crown. This can be caused by nematodes, fungus diseases, fertilizer burn, improper pesticide use, to name of few. Dieback isn't a natural part of the plant's growth pattern.

Doglegs are canes that grow at odd angles, often outward, then upward. This can be due to injury, the cane's attempt to reach for the sun or pruning practices.

Dolomite, or dolomitic lime, is a crushed limestone that can raise the pH level of the soil and add some magnesium. If it is to be used it should be mixed with the soil before planting, because a top dressing of lime percolates down into the soil very slowly.

Dormancy is the state of being dormant or inactive. Most plants native to regions where snow happens wisely take some time off and hibernate. There are some plants that go dormant in the summer, some that bloom in the spring and then disappear until next year. Perhaps we can learn a lesson from these plants and simply relax and enjoy some time off when the weather gets too rough for us.

Dormant plants are those that are on vacation. They have usually dropped their leaves, canceled all appointments, refuse to answer the telephone and are taking a long winter's nap. This is a rest period, and it is necessary for many plants and many types of roses that are native to more northern climes.

Double rose For a rosarian to see double the blossom must have 25 or more petals.

Downy mildew is a fungus disease that attacks during the cooler months when there is a good deal of humidity and poor air circulation. It begins as irregular purple splotches on the leaves and immature stems. Prevention by keeping the bush open to maintain proper air circulation is the best cure.

Dr. Huey is a red once-blooming rose that's popular as a rootstock in many parts of the United States, particularly Texas and California. It is usually considered the second choice for Florida roses with Fortuniana being the best for roses in the deep South. It isn't as effective in our sandy soil, nor is it as tolerant of our heat as Fortuniana.

Drip line If you were to trace a circle around your rose bush, or any other plants at the edge of the leaf canopy, this would be the drip line. It's the point at which the rain water runs off. Think of the bush as an umbrella and the drip line as the edge of that umbrella.

English roses, see David Austin Roses

Epsom salts or Magnesium sulfate is an excellent source of magnesium because it is in a safe form that plants can readably absorb. It is also a great addition to the gardener's bath water after a hard day in the rose garden.

Fertilizer banding is the placing of a plant food in bands around your plants and covering with soil or mulch, but not actually mixing it into the soil.

Florets are the individual flowers in a cluster of blossoms, such as those on a polyantha or floribunda rose.

Floribunda A group of roses created in the early part of the 20th century by crossing the traditional polyanthas with the relatively new hybrid teas. Most floribundas are shorter that hybrid teas with smaller flowers in clusters, called a candelabra or spray. Most floribundas are not known for their fragrance but they tend to be very *floriferous.*

Floriferous is a term used when referring to a plant, or variety, that tends to produce lots of flowers, or bloom in abundance.

DEFINING THE ROSE

Flower buds are a thing of immense beauty, with sensuous form and intoxicating fragrance, with elegance and charm, with both hope and promise. The rose bud is a symbol of all that is good in humanity, yet there is a touch of the sinful wrapped in the rosebud.

Flush is a term used in reference to the blooming habits of many roses. They tend to produce a great number of flowers all at once; this mass of blossoms is referred to as a flush. Then there is a rest period while new buds are formed and the plant gets ready for another flush. For once-blooming roses this flush occurs only once a year.

Foliar feeding is feeding through the leaves, usually with a weak solution of water-soluble nutrients. This was once a popular method of feeding, but many now argue that few of the nutrients are actually absorbed through the leaves. Most of it is absorbed by the roots when the spray drips off into the soil. These liquid fertilizers are effective as snack food for many plants and provide almost immediate gratification for the gardener, but the feast and famine nature of this feeding can open the door to a number of disease problems.

Fragrance Part of the ages old charm of the rose has been its intoxicating fragrance. Actually there is a great diversity in rose scents. They are usually classified as "old rose," "fruity," "spicy," "tea," or "musky." Some roses are far more fragrant than others and each of us perceives aromas differently, so what may be a rose with a beautiful fragrance to me, may have little or no scent at all to you. Roses are most fragrant in mid morning on a bright sunshiny day, but weather, temperature, stress factors can affect the amount of volatile oils produced. For the truly dedicated rose enthusiast, a bright, clear, warm, perfect day is sufficient reason to call off from work and spend the day smelling the roses. In fact we would all be healthier, both physically and mentally, if we paused in our mad pursuit of whatever it is we are madly pursuing at the moment and took time to smell the roses. Some of the most fragrant roses we grow are Belinda's Dream, Double Delight, Mr. Lincoln, Scentimental and Flo Nelson.

PART 5

Fungus Not all fungi are evil, sadistic predators that have dedicated their lives to terrorizing your choice roses. The vast majority of fungi are beneficial and absolutely necessary for root growth. In Florida we are faced with Blackspot, powdery mildew, and sometimes downy mildew. Everyone makes a big fuss over the fungus problems here, but Florida is free of many of the more serious disease problems that strike roses in the northern United States, Europe and the Orient. Fungus problems can be avoided easier than they can be cured. First, there are splendid rose varieties that are disease resistant, and new ones are being developed all the time. Planting in a sunny location, avoiding the tendency to over feed, providing good air circulation and good housekeeping will also help to prevent fungus problems from occurring, or getting out of hand.

Fungicide Usually, a chemical compound designed to kill, prevent, or at least slow down a specific fungus or groups of fungi. This is where we turn when we neglect the maintenance and care suggestions made above. Great care must be exercised when using fungicides because they can, if applied improperly, cause great harm to roses, nearby landscape plants, gardens, gardeners and their families, neighborhood children, pets and wildlife. These are poisons that can also do great harm to beneficial fungi that work for a living in the soil around your plants.

Gallica roses are antique roses originating in France. These pink or red flowers are noted for their intense fragrance. Most Gallica roses bloom once a year, but some are remonstrant.

Grafting is the way most named varieties of roses are propagated. By taking a bud from the desired variety and grafting in onto the root stock of a variety, such as Fortuniana, that is ideally suited for the conditions where the plant is to grow, a quality rose bush can be enjoyed.

Grandiflora roses are the result of a cross between Hybrid Teas and Floribundas. They are showy, producing large flowers in clusters. Queen Elizabeth is a popular grandiflora variety. There is some disagreement among experts as to whether or not this classification should continue.

Green manure is a cover crop of living plants that is grown to enrich the soil, first with its roots, by breaking up clay or adding organic matter in sandy types. Second the plants are tilled into the top layer of the soil to add humus or instant compost. Some of the choice cover crops are annual rye, clover and alfalfa. A cover crop that should be used more often is simple old green beans or black eyed peas.

Groundcover is a term applied to plants that form a dense covering that will control weeds and serve as a living mulch. In rose gardens some of the most effective ground covers include perennial peanut, chocolate mint and ivy.

Guard petals are the petals in the outer ring of a double flower. They serve as the protective layer for the inner petals, stamens and pistils before the bud opens. Guard petals are often streaked in green, a duller color or green at the base.

Gypsum, Calcium sulfate was popular with rose growers and was used as a soil additive in the days when every gardener mixed his or her own soils. It is still used in many commercial mixes, and you will find it recommended in many rose texts.

Hardening off can mean two different things to a rose enthusiast. We want the plants to harden off, or become better able to take the rigors of harsh weather, frosts, cold winds, etc. This is accomplished by not overfeeding, by being careful with the pruning and providing adequate water. For the rose grower who is displaying flowers at a rose show hardening off is the practice of placing the blossoms in water in a cool place, often under refrigeration for a few hours before putting them on display.

Hardy refers to a plant or variety that can withstand low temperatures. Rugged refers to a plant that can withstand a variety of conditions. Weed is a term used applied to plants that can survive in spite of us.

PART 5

Hips The real reason a rose bush produces flowers is to produce seeds. If you don't deadhead your roses you may find seedpods, that we call *hips*, forming. It should be noted that for some members of the rose family this is a very good thing. Apples, pears, peaches, plums, apricots, quinces and medlar (look it up) are all members of the big family that botanists refer to as *Rosaceae*. When allowed to go to seed many varieties of roses will cease blooming, or at least slow down. If you harvest the flowers for bouquets, or remove the spent blooms, this will encourage the plant to produce more flowers in a vain attempt to produce more seeds. Some rose hips are colorful in the winter, most of these are northern varieties where the red berries contrast well with the snow. Rose hips are a favorite snack for many birds, and there are also some varieties that people enjoy as a food item or as a source of vitamin C.

Honeydew is the clear sticky excreta of aphids, scale, mealybugs and white flies. This is a sugar rich material because it is what's left of the plant's sap after the bugs have digested what they need. Ants actually farm aphids, raising great herds of these miniature "cattle," defending them against predators like ladybugs, even taking them to new pastures when the population gets too large in one location. This honeydew drips onto the leaves below and becomes a great place for sooty mold to grow. To cure sooty mold eliminate the aphids.

Humus is simply the decayed plant or animal material in good soil. It is what compost dreams of becoming.

Hybrids are the result of a cross between two distinct varieties or species. The process involves taking the pollen from one variety and pollinating the flower of the other variety. The resulting seeds are then planted and the progeny are observed, tested, evaluated and most are discarded, but a few will have the desired traits and they are subjected to further trials.

Hybrid tea is a rose trend that began with the first hybrid, La France, developed in 1867, and has become the most popular class of roses on the market today. Hybrid Teas are noted for their large

DEFINING THE ROSE

flowers, one per stem, with that stem being sturdy, making the long-stemmed red rose the most popular flower in the world. There are several traits that make the Hybrid Tea welcome in the everyday gardener's backyard. They tend to be repeat or continuous bloomers. They have a beautiful bud form that makes the flower attractive even before it opens. In spite of the constant complaints, most Hybrid Teas are fragrant. They also come in a wide range of colors and shades to match a multitude of moods, themes and decors.

Inert material is the stuff that doesn't do anything. When you buy a bag of fertilizer or a container of pesticide you will find that most of what you bought was *inert material*. You think you got took, but it's for your own good, because if these chemicals were placed in the average gardener's hands in greater concentrations they would destroy the plants, the garden and probably, the gardener. They help make the chemicals safer and easier to use.

Inflorescence is a big word that refers to the flower stem, spike, spray or cluster that may exhibit one or a multitude of individual blossoms or florets. A single long stemmed red rose is an inflorescence, as is a spike of baby's breath.

Insecticide is a product created or designed to kill insects. Many insecticides are natural, often called organic, such as Neem and Pyrethrin. Others are petro-chemical derivatives such as Diazinon and Dursban. All must be used with caution. It is important to read the label and know the proper mixture to use and how to apply. It is even more important to actually follow those directions. Using a mixture that is too strong, applying when the temperature is too high or to the wrong plants can result in the death of the very plants you thought you were defending. In Florida, lizards are about the best insecticide we have, and they're free.

Insecticidal soap isn't what you need to have the cleanest insects in the neighborhood. This is one of the organic insect controls that uses sodium and potassium salts in combination with vegetable oils to smother and suffocate many of the soft bodied insects such as aphids. Unfortunately it's only partially effective against scale

PART 5

and most flying insects.

Japanese beetles are a Yankee thing. It is a beautiful metallic or copper colored beetle that enjoys roses even more than people do. When someone tells you that roses are more difficult to grow in Florida than up north, just smile and remind them of Japanese beetles. In rose gardens in the North they will gleefully devour the leaves, buds and flowers of every rose bush in sight, especially the polyanthas. Fortunately, these shiny little bugs don't like our Florida climate. *Note: When using pesticides and all garden chemicals, please carefully follow the directions.*

Lateral stems are the shoots that grow from the side of a cane rather that the terminal buds at the apex. These are the side shoots that make a fuller plant, but often create a dense condition where fungus diseases can gain a foothold.

Lawn is a term usually applied to areas of the landscape where the homeowner attempts to cultivate grass. This is generally a boring expanse of green that requires considerably more attention than roses, is far more expensive to maintain than roses, has no fragrance and demands far more water than roses. As the Florida gardeners and landscapers cope with the coming water shortage more of these expanses of grass will be replaced with beds and mass plantings of Carefree Roses.

Layering is one of nature's own methods of propagation that is used by many members of the rose family, including raspberries, blackberries and the native prairie rose. Either the stem or the tip of the stem can be bent down and covered or buried in the soil. Roots will form where there is contact with the soil and the process begins all over again. This is how briar patches grow.

Leaching is the loss of nutrients in the soil by the action of water percolating through it. With Florida's sandy soils dissolved nutrients leach beyond the root zone quickly.

Leafcutter bees are the cause of those mysterious circles cut in the leaves of roses and some other plants. These aren't the result of aliens from Mars, just a common member of the bee family trying to make a living by cutting circles of leaf to stuff in its nesting site where eggs have been laid on paralyzed insects that will serve as lunch for the bee offspring. The circles are used to separate the chambers and plug the entrance. This does no harm to the plant and makes an interesting topic of conversation at the dinner table.

Leafhoppers are small aphid cousins that suck the plant juices from the stems and tender new growth. They are called leafhoppers because they fly from leaf to leaf and it looks like they are hopping. They can be a problem because the can carry disease organisms from plant to plant.

Leaflets are the small leaf segments that make up a compound leaf. The typical rose leaf has five leaflets.

Lime is a soil additive usually made by grinding limestone. It is often used to raise the pH (sweeten) the soil and is a source of calcium. Some types of lime also contain magnesium.

Loam is properly a fertile soil that is a mixture of particle sizes. Loam can be classified in a number of ways, such as sandy loam or clay loam depending on which particle sizes dominate. Good loam will contain organic matter.

Lubers are those giant black and orange grasshoppers that begin as cute little demons devouring everything in sight as soon as they hatch. It only gets worse as they grow. Unfortunately they have few natural enemies, although blacksnakes will eat them. A heavy soled shoe is your best defense.

Magnesium (Mg) is a nutrient that is essential for green leaves and the formation of chlorophyl.

Macro nutrients, major elements usually considered the big three: Nitrogen (N), Phosphorous (P) and Potassium (K). Think of them as the major food groups for a plant. These are the elements listed first on the fertilizer container. Often these are the only nutrients listed, but while a plant requires more of these nutrients than the others, a balanced diet will include Calcium, Iron, Magnesium and the trace or minor elements.

Microclimates are formed in sheltered areas, hill tops or valleys, any location where special conditions either shelter from or expose plants growing there to weather extremes, drainage, temperatures, etc. Growing roses in the shelter of a wooden fence creates a micro climate that may well protect from cold winds, but will also limit the air circulation around the plants and open the door to fungus diseases.

Micro elements, micro-nutrients are the nutrients that are needed in minute or trace amounts. Think of them as the multi-vitamins for a plant. They include such elements as manganese, copper, boron, zinc, cobalt and others. Sometimes iron, calcium and magnesium will be included in this group in the packaged mixes.

Miniature roses are an informal class of roses that tend to have smaller flowers and leaves but resemble the full size roses in appearance. Many miniature roses will become sprawling shrubs unless kept pruned. Some have buds only slightly larger than grains of rice, some are free-flowering while others are only occasional bloomers. There are many varieties of these tiny roses but some will not perform well in Florida. Most miniature roses are grown from cuttings, and the root system isn't well suited for our soils and climate. They can be effectively grown as container plants but tend to be short lived.

Minor elements, see Micro elements

Mist propagation is a way of starting cuttings or growing on bud grafts by using an intermittent misting spray to maintain an optimum humidity and keep the cutting clean and free from disease organisms. This system is often used in enclosed areas, propagating cases and greenhouses.

Mites, properly spider mites, are spider kin, not true insects. They are so small that they are almost invisible. They come in a variety of colors and varieties. They colonize the underside of the leaf or groups of leaves and laugh at your inability to see them until it's too late. They will construct great tents of fine spider web material that protects their ever expanding communities from your sprays and the weather. Under these great tents they feed and reproduce with a wanton disregard for your efforts to grow beautiful show quality plants. Watch for leaves with a fine peppering of brown or black spots, a loss of the beautiful shine that is a part of rose foliage and in advanced stages the webs wrapping the leaves and new growth like a funeral shroud. There are organic sprays that are safe and provide control. There are also chemical sprays that can give a quicker kill but can pose a problem for both your health and the well being of the rose bush. Insects and predator mites feed on these destructive little critters, if we don't spray them into oblivion.

Miticide A chemical or organic material designed to control mites. Many of the chemical compounds are dangerous to people, pets and small children. his being the case, they are restricted to professional use by individuals licensed to use them. There are organic materials, pepper waxes, soaps, neem compounds and others that are safe for use by the everyday gardener.

Modern rose is a collective term used to distinguish the hybrid tea, floribunda and grandiflora roses that came into being after 1867 from the antique, traditional and old fashioned roses.

Modern shrub rose describes a rose developed in the late nineteenth or twentieth century that has the characteristics of the traditional, old fashioned or old shrub roses. Most of the modern shrub roses are repeat bloomers that are low maintenance.

Mulch is any material used around cultivated plants, applied between the soil surface and the atmosphere. This can be anything from pine needles to eucalyptus chips, crushed stone to brick chips, leaves, coffee grounds, porous fiber mats, old leisure suits or anything else that permits air and water to flow between the soil and the air. Mulch reduces the weed growth, keeps the soil temperature and moisture level even, reduces the water needs, and limits the spread of soil borne diseases and insects. Mulch is cheap, saves you labor, improves attractiveness of the rose garden and helps the rose bushes maintain their health and general vigor. You can also use low growing ground covers as a living mulch. Some of the creeping herbs also help to discourage some insects. Chives, spicy globe basil, chocolate mint and thyme all work well as a living mulch.

Multiflora rose is a weed rose that serves as a superior rootstock in the Northeast and much of Europe. It bears clusters of single white flowers and was used for some time as an erosion control but has a tendency to become invasive.

Nematodes are a problem you can't see. These critters are almost microscopic plant predators that live in the soil, invade your rose's roots and gradually kill the plant. They can be a serious problem for many rootstocks but Fortuniana doesn't seem to taste good to them. Working lots of organic material into the soil before planting also encourages fungi that feed on nematodes. Not all nematodes feed on your roses. As an example roundworms that attack your pets are nematodes. Not all nematodes are an evil force aligned against your garden, many are beneficial in that they feed on the bad guys including mites, insects and other nematodes.

Nematocides exist to kill nematodes. Several chemical formulas are available, but the best defense is to plant nematode resistant stock. There are nematodes on the market for farmers and home gardeners who wish to fight fire with fire. These are beneficial nematodes that feed on the bad guys that terrorize your roses.

Nitrogen is one of the big three nutrients a plant needs to thrive and grow. This is the first number in the nutrient formula listed on a container of plant food. It is the N in the N-P-K formula and is necessary for the production of healthy green leaves. While four-fifths of the atmosphere is composed of "free" nitrogen, your roses, and most other plants can't use it in this form. A lack of nitrogen results in limited growth, pale leaves and chlorosis. There is also a danger in applying too much nitrogen, because this can stimulate weak rampant growth with lots of disease prone leaves and fewer blossoms. A periodic application of a timed-release fertilizer like Osmocote provides a healthy amount of all the necessary nutrients.

Nitrogen fixation is conversion of the "free" nitrogen that's floating around in the air into compounds that plants can use. Much of this work is done by bacteria in the soil in the process of turning dead leaves and such into compost. Many beans and peas also employ bacteria to "fix" nitrogen. This is why alfalfa, perennial peanut and many other members of the bean family make such effective cover crops. Lightening is also effective in creating usable nitrogen oxides from the atmospheric nitrogen.

Nodes are the point on the stem where the leaves and buds form.

NPK is the collective chemical symbol for the three major elements in any complete plant food. **N** is a chemist's shorthand for Nitrogen, **P** is for Phosphorous and **K** is for Potassium.

Old roses are those roses that were grown and enjoyed in the garden before the rose revolution of 1867. These are also referred to as Old-fashioned roses, antique roses and traditional roses. There are several classes of these old roses, including Bourbons, Chinas, Damasks, Gallicas, Ramblers, Rugosas and the Tea rose (not Hybrid teas).

Old garden rose is another term for the old roses described above.

Once blooming roses are those that, logically enough, bloom once a year. This can be a massive, dramatic floral display and it will usually be in spring or early summer. Many of the antique or traditional roses are once blooming. It should be noted that these roses tend to produce these floral masterpieces in mature growth, so it is best to prune them soon after blooming. If you prune in the autumn or winter you may sacrifice some of the next season's display.

PART 5

Organic matter to the chemist simply refers to carbon compounds. To the everyday gardener it's a term applied to material that was once a part of a living organism, either plant or animal. This can range from peat moss to manure, fallen leaves to grass clippings, compost, mulch and humus. It makes use of natural recycling because when you use these once living materials in your rose bed, or any other gardening, they become a part of the new plants. This cycle continues in the form of new leaves, flowers and seeds.

Own root roses are grown as seedlings or rooted cuttings rather than grafted onto a root-stock. Many miniature and shrub roses are grown and sold on their own root. For most roses success in Florida is dependent on the Rosa Fortuniana rootstock. Some experts recommend own-root roses for use in decorative containers or raised beds only.

Packaged roses are those bare-root rose bushes sold with short, leafless, waxed canes in a plastic bag filled with sawdust or some other material. There is always a beautiful picture in the front of the package that serves as a suggestion of what may be inside. They often are sold in discount stores, grocery stores and non-garden center locations. They rarely give any clues as to the root-stock used. While they are far less expensive than container grown, Florida grown roses the chances for success are limited. They may well grow for a year or two, but the unsuitable rootstock will usually spell trouble and decline will claim the plant, regardless of what you do. Planting packaged roses is sorta like playing the lottery. We all know the odds, but we are all pathological optimists, so we buy the ticket anyway.

Patented roses are roses that have been "invented" by a hybridizer or grower. A plant patent gives the owner of the patent exclusive rights to distribute and/or propagate that plant for seventeen years. Patented roses usually cost more because the grower must pay for the rights to propagate it. It is illegal to reproduce a patented rose, or any other patented plant, even for your own personal use. Beware the Patent Police. Violating patent rights can result in serious fines.

Perlite is a soil additive and conditioner, that looks like little white snowflakes in the soil. It's made from a lighter than water volcanic rock called tuff. This mineral is crushed and heat treated to make it expand. It helps to aerate the soil, absorb water and encourage healthy roots.

Perpetual bloomer refers to a rose that is in flower over an extended period of time rather than for a short season.

Pesticides are either chemicals or organic materials designed to kill pests. Some are specific like insecticides that kill insects, or fungicides that kill fungi, or herbicides that kill, not herbs, but weeds. These are a valuable tool, but there must be caution applied when they are used. Remember that these are poisons designed to kill. Follow the directions, use caution, use common sense.

Petaloids are the small petals located in the center of the flower. When they appear in quantity they may conceal the stamens and give the bloom a fuller appearance.

Phosphorous is the nutrient important in the formation of healthy root growth and quality flower production. The proper amount is usually available in a timed release fertilizer and extra applications aren't necessary. Too much phosphorous can cause more problems than too little. In the **NPK** nutrient formula on the plant food container this is the **P**.

Photosynthesis is what a plant does for a living. Without green leaves working from sun up to sun down converting carbon dioxide, water, nutrients and sunlight into leaves, roots, flowers and seeds, we couldn't exist. This is done at the cell level with chlorophyll.

Pistil is the female reproductive organ of the flower.

Plant lice An insulting and derogatory term used when referring to aphids. For more information on these cattle of the insect world see *aphids*.

Pollen is the dust-like grains produced by the anthers of a flower. These are the male sex cells and their mission in life is to create seeds for the next generation. Rose pollen is rather heavy, thus is doesn't float through the air causing people with allergies to sneeze. It isn't the pollen that carries the fragrance of roses either. The scent of the rose is a volatile oil.

Polyantha roses are hardy and rugged old garden roses that tend to be dwarf in their growth habit with a profusion of small blooms, usually in clusters. The fragrance of most polyantha roses is light to mild. Polyanthas are the most widely used roses at Walt Disney World in Orlando. They make wonderful colorful plantings that are maintenance light.

Potassium is also called potash. In the plant food formula NPK, potassium is the K. It's needed for disease resistance, floral color and healthy roots and stems.

Powdery mildew is a fungus that forms a powdery white or gray coating on the top side of leaves and over young buds. This is a fungus that forms on dry leaves during periods of high humidity, hot days and cool nights. The best way to avoid this problem is to give your roses breathing room. Where there is good air circulation this fungus is less likely to become established. If you notice this fungus on your roses a tablespoon of baking soda in a gallon of water makes an effective and safe spray. Powdery mildew is more likely to find a home on crape myrtle than roses.

Prickles are what the purists call what everyone else refers to as thorns on a rose bush. Regardless of the technical or proper term for these defensive structures, we cannot print what they are usually called when we encounter them during a session of rose pruning.

pH is the symbol for the degree of acidity in the soil. The scale goes from a very acid **0** to totally alkaline **14**. Roses do best with a pH between 6.0 and 6.8.

Propagation is the way we produce new rose plants. The rose itself prefers the sexual method of reproduction, producing flowers that in turn produce seeds and a new generation. Because this is a lengthy process and the offspring may be uniquely different than the parents, growers prefer asexual methods of reproduction, at least for the roses. This can be in the form of cuttings struck in propagating cases or the more popular grafting of a scion or bud onto a rootstock. In Florida the most productive and long lived roses are those grafted onto *Rosa fortuniana* rootstock.

Pruning is the removal of damaged, weak or otherwise unnecessary growth to promote good health and a pleasant appearance. This is based on an understanding of how the rose grows as a plant and the wisdom of an experienced gardener, as opposed to the rest of us who are best classified as butchers.

Raised beds are created by using timbers, stone or other material to elevate a growing area above the soil line. This can also be achieved by mounding. The goal is to provide better drainage and greater control over the growing site.

Rambling roses are wannabe climbers, but they lack the determination. Too rampant and sprawling to be considered shrubs, they find themselves between these two growth forms.

Recurrent is a term rose experts use to show off when they want to describe a rose as a repeat bloomer, producing flowers in flashes throughout the year.

Registered roses are registered with the American Rose Society, which works with the International Registration Authority for Roses.

Remontant is a term used to describe a repeat or continuous blooming rose when recurrent doesn't seem snobbish enough. You can really impress your friends when you tell them your Belinda's Dream is remontant.

Repeat blooming roses are those that have some downtime between their showoff seasons. They are usually at their best in the spring and the fall and take some time off during our Florida summers.

Root bound plants have developed a root system that has outgrown the container. Because roses develop husky root systems, many varieties don't do well in containers as a permanent home.

Rootstock think *Rosa fortuniana.*

Root zone is a term applied to the top 12 to 24 inches of soil where the majority of a plants roots are growing. The root zone depth can vary with the plants being cultivated.

Rosaceae is what the botanists call the rose family. It includes strawberries, raspberries, apples, peaches, pears, quince and a multitude of other flowers, fruits and weeds.

Rose colored glasses have pink lenses to give us a rosey outlook. When used instead of Raybans we can all have a more optimistic attitude, smile at total strangers and approach life with unbridled joy.

Rugged plants are able to withstand harsh conditions, hard times, drought, floods, starvation, abusive pruning, overfeeding and keep on blooming. Hardy plants are those that can withstand cold weather.

Rust is a fungus disease that causes yellow spots on the top side of the leaf and rusty colored patches on the underside. Proper maintenance can help to prevent this disease, and can also prevent the spread if it does occur.

Scale is really an aphid in a suit of armor. These sucking insects

DEFINING THE ROSE

hide under the leaves or along the stems of your prize rose.

Scions are the buds grafted onto the rootstalk. This is what grows into the rose you know and love while all the work is done by the rootstalk.

Semi-double rose blooms usually have between 12 and 24 petals.

Sepals are the modified green leaves that cover the flower bud before it opens.

Shrub roses, also "modern shrub roses," are often divided into large-flowered, cluster-flowered and polyanthas. Crosses have resulted in a great deal of confusion about paternity, and classification, but the named ones are there for us all to enjoy.

Single roses are roses with flowers displaying 5 to 12 petals.

Slow release fertilizers release their nutrients gradually. Because of this there is less danger of fertilizer burn. It's also far easier to apply some Osmocote twice a year that a liquid plant food every two weeks. It is also cheaper and requires no special sprayers or applicators. Some of these slow release plant foods are called timed release.

Sooty mold is the black velvet coating that forms on leaves growing under an infestation of aphids, mealy bugs, scale or any other sucking insect. This sooty mold isn't attractive, but it does little damage, or at least, not as much as the insects above. The mold is growing on the honeydew, or excreta from the bugs. It has a high sugar content and that is what the mold is growing on, not the plant.

Species roses are wild roses, unchanged by rose growers. These are the only roses that will grow true from seed. Multiflora is one example.

Specimen when we are talking about roses, refers to any stem that terminates in a flower or group of flowers. For Olympic athletes it has a different meaning.

Spider mites see mites

Sport is a term used by botanists for a genetic mutation that occurs without the intervention of the grower or hybridizer. A sport can be in color variation, vigor, leaf form or growth habit.

Spray is a cluster or group of florets on a single main stem.

Spreader sticker is the material added to pesticides to make them adhere to the leaves, even after a rain.

Spurs refer to the short growth that matures before it forms a bud. This is often a result of weather, drought or cold.

Stamens are the male reproductive organs of the flower that produce the pollen. The thread-like structure is called the filament. On the top of this filament is the anther that contains the pollen.

Standard roses are roses trained to tree form. When purchasing tree roses try some of the Carefree roses as a choice. They will preform very well for you.

Stems are the plant parts that produce the leaves. In roses the stems are called canes and they are located between the roots and the flowers.

Stress external factors that impede our proper functioning, interfere with our mental and physical health, and in general rob us of our sense of well-being. In roses stress is the result of external forces that deny the plant an opportunity to be all that it can be. These stresses can be in the form of heat, cold, drought, overfeeding or pesticides.

Suckers are canes that grow from below the graft. They are a vigorous attempt by the rootstock to take over the entire plant. These

DEFINING THE ROSE

shoots usually will have different shaped leaves and grow much faster than the desirable top growth. They should be removed unless you are exceedingly curious to see what a Fortuniana flower looks like. If it is a rose that was started from a cutting and is growing on its own root there is no need to remove this growth.

Systemic refers to a pesticide that works through the plant's system, rather that only the surface.

Thrips are minute little insects that set out to destroy the rose flower by devouring it in the bud stage. They prefer light colored flowers so that the brown spots that result from their acts of sabotage are most visible. Hummingbirds and a number of insects feed on the thrips. They can also be controlled with a number of insecticides.

Top-dressing refers to the application of mulch, compost, or fertilizer to the soil surface rather that digging it in. Top-dressing is much easier on the gardener and doesn't disturb the roots of your pet roses.

Transpiration is the way a plant breathes. The moisture absorbed by the roots, has flowed through the plant to the leaves and is returned into the cosmos through the pores. Along with the water vapor, oxygen is also released.

Tree rose see standard rose

Turgid describes plant cells containing the proper amount of moisture. Each cell is like a micro-balloon. When turgid the cell is firm and the foliage is erect. Wilting occurs when there is insufficient moisture available in the plant's system.

Vermiculite is a heat treated mineral called mica. It is used as a soil additive to increase water retention and encourage root development. Vermiculite is often a key ingredient in quality prepared soil mixes.

PART 5

Water is important to roses everywhere, but in Florida's sandy soils it becomes critical. This is one of the advantages of the Fortuniana rootstock. It develops a deep fibrous root system that can harvest more available water. It is also more drought tolerant that most other root stocks. Generally speaking, about one inch of water per week will keep your roses happy. A good surface mulch also helps.

Water soluble fertilizers are also called fast release or quick release fertilizers. The nutrients are in chemical combinations that literally melt in water and are immediately available to the plant. The liquid and foliar plant foods are all water soluble, as are the cheap bagged fertilizers. This is snack food for your plants. It provides a burst of growth, then no more food is available and the plant becomes stressed. It is easy to overfeed with these plant foods. It's better for the plants and easier for you to use slow-release or timed release plant foods like Osmocote or Sta-Green.

Rose trivia:

The oldest living rose may well be a 1000-year-old bush that grows against a wall of the Hildesheim Cathedral in Germany.

Shakespeare mentions or alludes to roses more than fifty times in his literary works.

The floors of Cleopatra's palace in Egypt were covered with fragrant rose petals. It was rumored that she slept on a mattress of rose petals as well.

The world's largest rose bush is in Tombstone, Arizona. The trunk is almost six feet in circumference. It covers an arbor where there is seating for more than 100 people. It was planted from a cutting started more than 150 years ago. This is a Lady Banks rose. Fortuniana is thought to be a sport of this rose or a cross between it and the Cherokee.

DEFINING THE ROSE

Rose Fact:

Try a rose in place of mistletoe. The biggest difference is that the rose works year round. Trust me.

Everything's Comin' Up Roses in the Music Industry

There's a multitude of songs written about roses, which use the rose as a metaphor, or have roses in their titles. The following are only a few of the most popular. If we include different languages and cultures the list is well over four thousand long. How many of these do you remember?

Nat King Cole sang of the *Ramblin' Rose* as a musical metaphor, and Jim Reeves waxed poetic with *Roses are Red, Violets Are Blue*.

On the wild side we have *To a Wild Rose* and *My Wild Irish Rose*. Speaking of Irish roses we have *Rose of Killarney* and *The Rose of Tralee*. The Irish have been particularly enthusiastic about roses with even more classics including the beautiful ballad, *The Banks of the Roses*. These Irish romantics also gave us *My Lovely Rose of Clare* and *Sweet Rosie O'Grady*. Tommy Sands gave us the powerfully poetic and incredibly sad Irish ballad about the religious conflict that tore friends and families apart, *There Were Roses*.

We had *Only a Rose*, and then there was *Second Hand Rose*. Not to mention Franky Lane's impassioned declaration, *Rose, Rose, I Love You*.
The teeny-boppers danced to *Roses & Lollipops* while Bobby Darren sang about *Sixteen Yellow Roses*. Then we can fast forward to the hard rock of Guns & Roses and their album, *Stolen Roses*.

That takes us out west to the *Yellow Rose of Texas*, a song about a lady who kept Santa Anna occupied while the Texans were getting in position for the Battle of San Jacinto. We also have *San Antonio*

PART 5

Rose and *Mexicali Rose*.

Henry Mancini's *Days of Wine & Roses* is one of the all time classic love songs as was — *Moonlight and Roses*.

Roger Whitiker made the Christmas song *Mighty Like a Rose* a seasonal tradition. We also have the classic hymn, *Lo 'ere a Rose Is Blooming*.

I Never Promised You a Rose Garden but there were roses at Ricky Nelson's *Garden Party*.

The songs got colorful *When She Wore a Tulip, I Wore a Red, Red Rose*. Staying with Crayola music, who could forget *Red Roses for a Blue Lady*? Tammy Graham sang a beautiful song about *A Dozen Red Roses* delivered to a young lady on her wedding day from her father who had passed away.

Primrose Lane isn't really about roses but we threw it in this list anyway.

Nelson Eddie sang his heart out to *Rose Marie* and Bette Midler gave us *The Rose*. There was *Rose of Washington Square* and *The Last Rose of Summer*.

Enough of this. We didn't even mention Guns & Roses. You can probably think of dozens more, like Neil Diamond's *Cracklin' Rose*. It makes a great conversation starter for a garden party.

About the Author

Mark Nelson grew up in a rose garden. He was raised in Apopka, Florida, the home of Nelsons' Florida Roses, a division of O. F. Nelson & Sons Nursery. O.F. Nelson & Sons Nursery was founded by Mark's grandfather, Olin Nelson, and his two sons, B. P. And Earl Nelson. This nursery has been growing and selling roses since about 1960. B.P. and Earl were the innovators in the production of roses on Fortuniana rootstock. Nelsons' Florida Roses is far and away the largest grower of Fortuniana roses in the world today.

Mark worked at the nursery from the time he was old enough to weed. At some point he achieved a promotion to the rose fields. Mark attended Presbyterian College in Clinton, S.C. After graduation and service in the Army he returned to the family business for good in 1977.

Mark has been involved in all aspects of the nursery and currently serves as president. His cousin, Scott Nelson, is the general manager. Nelsons' Florida Roses is the result of stubborn hard work and dedication. Mark is proud of his staff and tells me that his employees are the finest, most experienced and dedicated in the nursery business, anywhere.

Hank Bruce

Photo identification and photography credits

Front cover
    Belinda's Dream — Tomi Jill Folk

Back cover
Left side, top to bottom
    Carefree Wonder — Roger Kilgore
    Louis Phillipe — Roger Kilgore
    Elina — Tomi Jill Folk
    Knock Out — Tomi Jill Folk
    Pink Summer Snow — Tomi Jill Folk
At right
    Don Juan — Tomi Jill Folk

Photo of Mark Nelson by Beth Nelson
Interior photos by Tomi Jill Folk
Interior line drawings by Hank Bruce

Hank Bruce, who collaborated on this book, is the author, most recently, of *Global Gardening*, distributed by Mickler's Books, Inc.

For additional copies of this book, visit your independent garden center or bookseller. For the dealer nearest you, visit www.micklers.com.